Mark Water

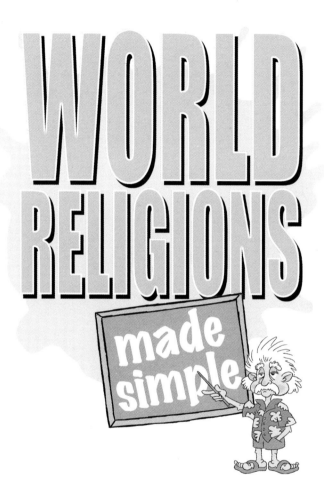

WORLD RELIGIONS
made simple

AMG
Publishers

God's Word is our highest calling.

AMG Publishers
6815 Shallowford Road
Chattanooga, Tennessee 37421

Copyright © 2002 John Hunt Publishing Ltd
Text © 2002 Mark Water

ISBN 0-89957-432-7

Designed by Andrew Milne Design

Printed in China.

Contents

Introduction

Understanding each other's faith

Never before has there been such an acute need to understand and respect the religious beliefs of other people. Clearly, caricatures of other religions have no place in the twenty-first century. At the very least, is it not reasonable to expect followers of different religions to live in harmony with each other? If we are to respect our neighbor who has a different faith; if we are to show courtesy towards such a person; if we are to share the insights of our own faith; and if we engage in evangelism we need to have a basic understanding of the different world faiths.

The need for knowledge

The first thing that is needed is for us to understand the teaching of other religions. This volume looks at the history, the founders, the teachings, the worship and the influence of all the major religions in the world.

The four larger world religions – Christianity, Islam, Hinduism and Buddhism – which account for probably as many as 87% of all those who have any religious faith, are discussed in some depth with examples from their sacred writings and quotations from their spiritual leaders.

The nearly 50 million adherents of Judaism, Sikhism, the Baha'i Faith, Jainism, and Shintoism, though smaller in numbers, are not overlooked and their origins, beliefs and influence today are explored.

A chapter on animism and primal religions then follows and makes a most interesting contrast with the next chapter which is about those who are influenced by and follow, consciously, or unconsciously, New Age ideas.

While atheists and agnostics have generally been in the minority, (about 4% of the world population, with about 240 millions adherents) their ideas have been promoted most aggressively and have often assumed an influence out of all proportion to their numbers. Many of the pro-abortion and pro-euthanasia lobbies bear eloquent testimony to this. And as more countries are becoming increasingly secular, an understanding of the basic tenets of existentialism, Marxism, skepticism, and secular humanism are important as never before.

The threat to world peace

Where religions allow or even encourage violence towards heretics or members of a different faith, individuals are not at liberty to walk the streets in safety. If terrorists are allowed to urge followers of Islam to enter into a jihad or holy war against the USA (and all infidels with impunity), world peace is seriously threatened. One of the clear messages from the events of September 11, 2001 is that fanaticism, dressed up in religious clothes, puts world peace in jeopardy. A sympathetic understanding of the world's religions can help to prevent this, as can making a distinction between the official teaching of a religion and the corrupt teaching of a splinter group of that religion. Ignorance about and fear of other people's religions only increases suspicion and antagonism between followers of different religions.

The quest for truth

Each religion seeks for the truth in its beliefs and worship. No religion worthy of the name of religion is frightened of the truth. Believers in every religion or world-view have the right to promote (but not to force) their beliefs. Today we have sufficient information about all the religions in the world to enable us to make informed, intelligent decisions about what we should believe. The

peace of the world and the eternal destiny of our souls is at stake.

Statistics

It is hard, if not impossible, to be precise about how many people belong to each world religion. However, there are some general facts and figures that are not in dispute.

The big five

For the past 100 years scholars of comparative religion have increasingly recognized Judaism, Christianity, Islam, Hinduism, and Buddhism as the most significant world religions, and they are still thought of as the "Big Five."

WORLD RELIGIONS COMPARED			
These figures assume a world population of 6 billion (6,000,000,000) at the turn of the second millennium.			
Religion	*%*	*Million*	*Comment*
Christianity (every group who upholds Jesus Christ in some way or form)	33	2,000	Includes Roman Catholics, Protestants, Eastern Orthodox, Pentecostals, Mormons, Jehovah's Witnesses, and nominal Christians
Islam	22	1,300	
Hinduism	15	900	
Non-religions	14	840	Includes atheists, agnostics, those who say they have no religion, and secular humanists
Buddhism	6	360	
Chinese religions	4	240	
Primal and indigenous	3	180	
Other religions	3	180	

1 *CHRISTIANITY*

Introduction

Christians and decline

Countless Christians and hundreds of Christian organizations are dedicated to carrying out Christ's final command to "make disciples of all nations" (Matthew 28:19). Revivals break out on every continent. Consequently, each year there is an overall increase in the number of people throughout the world who claim to be Christian.

However, the population of the world is increasing at an even faster rate and in the light of that, the Christian Church is in decline. The projection for the year 2010, based on current trends, indicates just how much ground Christians are losing.

In 1960, with a world population of 3 billion people, 30% professed the Christian faith.

By 1990, with a world population of 5.3 billion, this was reduced to 29%.

If present trends continue, in 2010, when the world population is expected to be 7 billion, only 27% of these people will be Christians.

Christianity, for so long the dominant faith in the world, is about to be overtaken by the "fastest growing religion in the world."

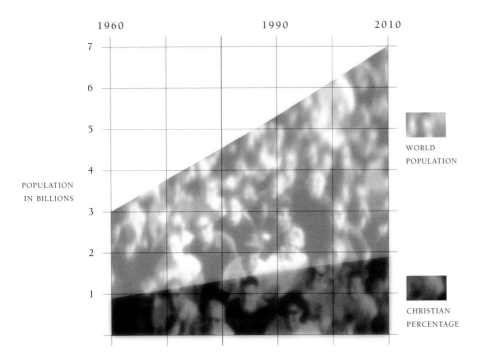

1960   1990   2010

POPULATION
IN BILLIONS

7
6
5
4
3
2
1

WORLD
POPULATION

CHRISTIAN
PERCENTAGE

Origins of Christianity

Christianity is founded on the life and teachings of Jesus Christ (4BC - 30AD), a Jew who was born in Bethlehem in the small district of Judea, part of the Roman province of Syria.

A summary of Jesus' life

The story about Jesus is recorded in the four accounts called Gospels - Matthew, Mark, Luke and John.

TIME-LINE OF LIFE OF JESUS CHRIST	
JESUS' BIRTH AND CHILDHOOD	
4 BC	Jesus is born.
3 BC	Joseph, Mary and Jesus flee to Egypt.
2 BC	Joseph, Mary and Jesus settle in Nazareth.
AD 8	The 12-year-old Jesus astounds the Jewish teachers in the Temple with his understanding.
THE MINISTRY OF JESUS (1) AD27 A YEAR OF OBSCURITY	
AD 27	The baptism and temptations of Jesus.
THE MINISTRY OF JESUS (2)AD 28 A YEAR OF POPULARITY	
AD 28	Jesus chooses the 12 apostles.
AD 28	Jesus preaches the Sermon on the Mount.
THE MINISTRY OF JESUS (3) AD29 A YEAR OF CONTROVERSY	
AD 30	Jesus is crucified, rises from the dead, and, after 40 days, ascends into heaven.

Birth and childhood

Mary, a village girl from Nazareth in the Galilee hills, was engaged to be married to a carpenter, Joseph. The angel Gabriel told her that she would give birth to a baby son and that her baby, who had been conceived by the power of God, would be a great king. Jesus was born in a barn or cave in Bethlehem. He grew up in the village of Nazareth and became a carpenter like his father.

Jesus' work begins

Later, Jesus' cousin, John the Baptist appeared in the desert proclaiming the imminent arrival of the long-awaited Deliverer (the Messiah). Jesus (now about 29 years old) came down from Nazareth and joined the crowds waiting to be baptized by John. At his baptism the Holy Spirit descended upon him and a voice from heaven said, "You are my son, whom I love."

The Spirit led Jesus into the desert where he spent 40 days fasting and praying. During this time he was tempted to use his powers for worldly, selfish and devilish ends

Rejecting the temptation, Jesus emerged from the desert to begin a three year ministry of teaching and healing accompanied by a motley group of 12 "apostles," whom he called to be with him.

Jesus' teaching and work

Jesus proclaimed the "good news" that the kingdom, the rule, of God had now arrived. He often spoke in parables, hiding his message so that his words had to be explained to his disciples.

His many miracles of healing not only revealed his deep love for suffering people, but were signs that he himself was the Messiah whose coming had been described in the Jewish Scriptures.

Through the ages many have read into the teaching and actions of Jesus a multitude of things. He has been seen as anything from a Che Guavera type of freedom fighter to a mystical pacifist. What is certain is that he turned human values upside down and taught a message of communion with God, who is a loving Father and friend to people in need. He taught the urgency of refusing all greed, arrogance and lovelessness, and said that following him opened the way to a life of freedom and peace with the one eternal God.

Opposition to Jesus

During his time many thousands of people flocked to Jesus hoping he would be the leader who would throw out the Romans. The Sadducees, the aristocratic rulers in Jerusalem, began to see him as a threat to the stability of the country.

At a major Jewish festival in Jerusalem one of his own disciples, Judas, betrayed him to a contingent of soldiers who captured Jesus at night, and within the space of a few hours he was hurriedly condemned so he could be immediately crucified. He was buried but after three days he arose alive. He appeared to his friends and ate bread and fish to emphasize the reality of his resurrection.

His life on earth concluded, when after 40 days he ascended to be with God the Father.

"He was taken before their very eyes" Acts 1:9.

He told his apostles before his ascension to preach his message throughout the world and promised to return in glory to judge humankind on the basis of their obedience to his words.

Christian beliefs

Christianity's beliefs are based on the teachings contained in the Bible.

Beliefs about God

- there is only one God
- God created the world and is distinct from the world
- God is active within the world
- Humans are responsible to God for how they live
- Jesus Christ, the Son of God and equal with God, came to earth as a human being and died and rose again so that humankind might be reconciled to God.

The Trinity

God reveals himself in three "persons" (see Matthew 28:19):

- Father
- Son (Jesus Christ) and
- Holy Spirit.

These three persons are a unity, sharing one substance.

Jesus Christ: fully human, fully divine

Christians believe that although Jesus was fully God he was also fully human.

The death and resurrection of Christ

Jesus was executed by crucifixion, a painful and degrading execution, reserved for criminals. Christians believe that Jesus rose from the dead (the resurrection) after his execution and was seen by many people before he ascended into heaven.

It is believed that through faith in Jesus' death and resurrection, men and women can be restored to their correct relationship with God (see Ephesians 2:4-9).

The example of Christ

Christians believe they should live according to the example of Jesus Christ by:

- loving God (see Mark 12:30)
- loving fellow human beings as one loves oneself (see Matthew 19:19)
- sharing the Christian message (see Acts 1:8).

Judgment

Christians do not believe in reincarnation. After death everyone is judged by God.

"Just as man is destined to die once, and after that to face judgment."
Hebrews 9:27

Creeds

Christian creeds (the Latin word *credo* means "I believe") give condensed summaries of Christian belief.

The best known and earliest creed is the Apostles' Creed, so-called because the early church thought that it summed up the teaching of the apostles, not because it was written by the apostles. Similar creeds have been traced back to the end of the second century, but the form in which it is known goes back to the sixth century.

The Apostles' Creed

I believe in God,
the Father Almighty,
Maker of heaven and earth;
and in Jesus Christ
who was conceived by the Holy Spirit,
    born of the Virgin Mary,
suffered under Pontius Pilate,
was crucified, dead and buried;
he descended into hell:
on the third day he rose again from
    the dead;
he ascended into heaven and sits on
    the right hand of God the Father
    Almighty;
from there he will come to judge the
    living and the dead.
I believe in the Holy Spirit,
the holy catholic [universal] Church;
the communion of saints;
the forgiveness of sins;
the resurrection of the body,
and the life everlasting.

F.A.Qs

Q: What do the letters AD, BC, BCE and CE stand for?

A: The dating system the Romans used was based on the beginning of their community, AUC (*ab urbe condita* – "from the founding of the city [of Rome]"). In the sixth century an obscure monk, Abbot Dionysius Exiguus, replaced the Roman system with a new method that centered on Jesus Christ whom he saw as the "hinge of history." Exiguus calculated that the beginning of the Christian era was 754 years from the founding of Rome.

After this, Christians dated events BC (before Christ) and AD (*anno Domini* – "in the year of our Lord").

This dating system, introduced in AD 525, became accepted throughout the world. In deference to the sensitivities of followers of other religions it is now often replaced with BCE ("before the common era") and CE ("common era").

Baptism

Christian worship

Christians worship in a variety of places. In the first century they met together in each other's homes.

Today, Christians continue to meet in homes as well as in community or school halls, in churches and in cathedrals consecrated for worship. Worship services comprise hymns, prayers, readings from the Bible often with a sermon and affirmations of faith.

The Christian year

The two most important Christian festivals are:

- Easter, celebrating Jesus' resurrection, held on the last week of March or in April
- Christmas, celebrating Jesus' birth, always on December 25.

Sacraments

Sacraments are outward and visible signs of inward and spiritual gifts of God. Augustine called them "visible words." According to Orthodox and Roman Catholics, there are seven sacraments:

- baptism,
- confirmation,
- penance,
- the Mass,
- marriage,
- anointing the sick (extreme unction)
- and ordination.

Protestant churches believe that there are only two ordinances, which are sometimes called the Gospel sacraments:

- the Lord's Supper
- and baptism.

Baptism
1. Who should be baptized?

Christians hold different views about baptism.

Some Christians believe that only people old enough to make a witness about their personal faith in Christ should be baptized, preferably by total immersion in water.

Some Christians believe that children of believing parents should be baptized (that is consecrated water is poured over, or dabbed on the forehead, on which the sign of the cross may be made) as infants.

Some Christians believe that all children should be baptized as infants.

2. What does Christian baptism mean?

Baptism stands for:

- identification with Christ in his death and resurrection (see Romans 6:3-4)
- cleansing from sin (see Acts 2:38)
- the coming of the Holy Spirit to the person being baptized (see Titus 3:5).

When babies or young children are baptized, the parents, godparents and/or the members of the church congregation make promises on behalf of the child.

The Lord's Supper

Bread and wine

For many Christians, the Lord's Supper (also called the Eucharist, Holy Communion, the Mass) is at the heart of their faith. It comprises eating a small piece of bread or a wafer and, for Protestants, drinking from the fruit of the vine, with other Christians in a spirit of repentance and prayer.

The Lord's command

Christians do this because they believe that they are carrying out Christ's own command as they do so. At the Lord's Supper, which Jesus inaugurated on the eve of his crucifixion, he said, "Do this in remembrance of me." *Luke 22:19*

The apostle Paul described and explained the Lord's Supper in his letter to the Christians at Corinth (see 1 Corinthians 11:23-26).

Four views about the Lord's Supper

The four views which have unhappily divided the Christian world on the subject of the sacrament are the following:

1. The Romish [Roman Catholic] doctrine or transubstantiation

This maintains the absolute change of the elements into the actual body and blood of Christ so that, though the elements of bread and wine remain present to the senses, they are no longer what they seem being changed into the body, blood and divinity of Christ.

2. The Lutheran view called consubstantiation

This maintains that after consecration the body and blood of Christ are substantially present, but nevertheless, that the bread and wine are present yet unchanged.

3. The Anglican view

This view states that Christ is present in the sacrament only after the spiritual manner. His body and blood are eaten by the faithful after a spiritual not carnal manner. The focus is on the maintenance of one's spiritual life and growth in grace.

4. The Zwinglian vew

The Zwinglian view declares the sacrament to be not a channel of grace, but only a commemorative feast, admitting only a figurative presence of Christ's body and blood.

"Alas! that prisons should have been peopled, and thousands immolated on the pyre, for the sake of opinions."
John Foxe, The Book of Martyrs

WHAT ARE THE CHRISTIAN SYMBOLS?

- The cross is the symbol of Christianity. It is an empty cross and does not have the figure of Jesus on it to indicate he has risen from the dead.
- The crucifix, a cross with an image of Jesus crucified on it, is also used as a symbol for Christianity.

The Bible

The Bible is the Christian's holy book. It is divided into the Old Testament, which incorporates the Hebrew Bible, and the New Testament, which details the life and teachings of Jesus and the teachings of his apostles.

Protestant and Roman Catholic Bibles

Protestant Bibles do not include the books known as the Apocrypha, or Deuterocanon, which form part of Roman Catholic Bibles.

The Reformers did not include the apocryphal books as part of the divinely inspired Bible and said of them: "The other books, as Jerome has said, the church reads for example of life and instruction of manners; but yet doth it not apply them to establish any doctrine." *Article VI of the Church of England's Articles of Religion*

The Old Testament

The Old Testament is divided into four sections:

1. The five books of the Pentateuch

Genesis, Exodus, Leviticus, Numbers, Deuteronomy.

2. The 12 historical books

Joshua, Judges, Ruth, 1 and 2 Samuel, 1 and 2 Kings, 1 and 2 Chronicles, Ezra, Nehemiah, Esther.

3. Five poetical books

Job, Psalms, Proverbs, Ecclesiastes, Song of Songs.

4. 17 prophetic books

Five major prophets: Isaiah, Jeremiah, Lamentations, Ezekiel, Daniel.

12 minor prophets: Hosea, Joel, Amos, Obadaiah, Jonah, Micah, Nahum, Habakkuk, Zephaniah, Haggai, Zechariah, Malachi.

These prophetic books were first called "minor" in the fourth century AD, not because they are unimportant, but because they are much shorter in length than the five "major" prophets.

Inspiration

Christians believe that both the Old Testament and New Testament are inspired by God in a unique way so that the ultimate author of the Bible is God, even though it was written down by human writers. Two key Bible texts about the Bible's inspiration are:

- Peter 1:21 "for prophecy never had its origin in the will of man, but men spoke from God as they were carried along by the Holy Spirit."

- Timothy 3:16 "All Scripture is God-breathed…"

The New Testament
The New Testament falls into five sections:

1. Four biographical books
The four Gospels of Matthew, Mark, Luke and John record more about Jesus than any other books.

2. One historical book
Acts has been called "The Acts of the Apostles" and "The Acts of the Holy Spirit."

3. 13 letters of the apostle Paul
The 13 New Testament letters which are traditionally thought to have been penned by Paul, are Romans, 1 and 2 Corinthians, Galatians, Ephesians, Philippians, Colossians, 1 and 2 Thessalonians, 1 and 2 Timothy, Titus, and Philemon.

4. Eight non-Pauline letters
Nobody knows who wrote the letter of Hebrews, but the other letters bear the names of James, Peter (2 letters) and Jude. The other three short letters are traditionally ascribed to John the apostle.

5. One prophetic book
The book of Revelation was also written by a "John" who is also traditionally thought to be the writer of John's Gospel and three very short New Testament letters.

The canon
The Old Testament
The Christian church accepted the Hebrew Bible (the scriptures of Judaism) as its own scriptures as they were stamped with Christ's approval. Christ viewed these scriptures as the voice of God and Christians have always held to the same view about them.

The New Testament
The word "canon" is derived from a Greek word meaning a "reed" or "cane." In classical Greek this refers to a straight rod or carpenter's rule. When this word is applied to Scripture it refers to the "rule" of faith and truth. So the New Testament canon refers to those books which comprise the rule of faith which is the yardstick for belief and behavior for all time. These books were acknowledged by the church to be inspired scripture. Each book had to be written by an apostle of Jesus, or by a person who was part of the apostolic circle.

The Eastern Church first formally acknowledged our present list of New Testament books in AD 367 in Athanasius' Thirty-ninth Paschal Letter. The Western Church did the same in a conciliar decision in AD 397 at Carthage.

Early Christian leaders

Peter
?–c.AD 65

After the first followers of Christ were deprived of his physical presence Peter, one of Jesus' first disciples, became a leader in the Christian church.

In the first recorded Christian sermon, which resulted in 3,000 people becoming Christians, Peter said,

"Men of Israel, listen to this: Jesus of Nazareth was a man accredited by God to you by miracles, wonders and signs, which God did among you through him, as you yourselves know. This man was handed over to you by God's set purpose and foreknowledge, and you, with the help of wicked men, put him to death by nailing him to the cross. But God raised him from the agony of death, because it was impossible for death to keep its hold on him." *Acts 2:22-24*

Paul
c. AD 1–?65

The ex-rabbi's moment of encounter with the risen Christ is recorded three times in the Acts of the Apostles: Acts 9:1-19; 22:4-16; 26:9-18.

13 of the letters of the New Testament are traditionally ascribed to Paul, who also spent his life as a pioneer Christian missionary, before he was martyred, possibly with Peter in Rome, in AD 65.

Paul emphasized that religion is not a matter of keeping rules, that God opposes discrimination on the grounds of gender, race or class, and that we are saved by grace through faith in Jesus.

"Like the rest, we were by nature objects of wrath. But because of his great love for us, God, who is rich in mercy, made us alive with Christ even when we were dead in transgressions–it is by grace you have been saved. And God raised us up with Christ and seated us with him in the heavenly realms in Christ Jesus, in order that in the coming ages he might show the incomparable riches of his grace, expressed in his kindness to us in Christ Jesus. For it is by grace you have been saved, through faith–and this not from yourselves, it is the gift of God–not by works, so that no one can boast." *Ephesians 2:3-9*

After the apostles

In addition to the apostles, many great Christian leaders made crucial contributions to the life of the Christian church in later centuries. Men like Augustine, Benedict and Francis of Assisi were highly influential and godly Christians.

Ignatius of Antioch
?AD–?107

The third bishop of Antioch in Syria wrote seven letters on his way to his martyrdom in Rome, a collection which has been called "one of the most beautiful treasures bequeathed by the second-century church."

"Father, make us more like Jesus. Help us to bear difficulty, pain, disappointment and sorrow, knowing that in your perfect working and design

you can use such bitter experiences to mold our characters and make us more like our Lord. We look with hope to the day when we will be completely like Christ, because we will see him as he is. …I am God's wheat. May I be grounded by the teeth of the wild beasts until I become the fine wheat bread that is Christ's. My passions are crucified, there is no heat in my flesh, a stream flows murmuring inside me; deep down in me it says: Come to the Father."

Ignatius of Antioch, prior to his martyrdom

Justin Martyr
c. 100–c. 165

Justin Martyr was probably the most important early Christian Apologist (one who offered a reasoned defense). St Bernard said that Justin was, "the first thinker after St Paul to grasp the universalistic element in Christianity and to sum up in one bold stroke the whole history of civilization as finding its consummation in Christ."

Justin himself wrote, "No one makes us afraid or leads us into captivity as we have set our faith on Jesus. For though we are beheaded, and crucified, and exposed to beasts and chains and fire and all other forms of torture, it is plain that we do not forsake the confession of our faith, but the more things of this kind which happen to us the more are there others who become believers and truly religious through the name of Jesus." *Justin Martyr*

Origen
c. 185–254

Origen proved to be the best Christian theologian of the first half of the third century. When he was only 17 his father was martyred. He spent his life refuting the Roman authorities and in defending the Christian faith against heretics and the Jews.

Referring to the atonement, Origen wrote, "If there be no sin, the Son of God would not have had to become a lamb, nor would he have had to become incarnate and be put to death."

Basil the Great
c. 330–379

Basil was responsible for encouraging community life among monks rather than solitary asceticism and for emphasizing that monks should care for the poor and sick. He is therefore looked on as the founder of the idea of the monastic life.

In his battle against worldliness, Basil wrote, "We must try to keep the mind in tranquility. For just as the eye which constantly shifts its gaze, now turning to the right or to the left, now incessantly peering up or down, cannot see distinctly what lies before it, but the sight must be fixed firmly on the object in view if one would make his vision of it clear; so too man's mind when distracted by his countless worldly cares cannot focus itself distinctly on the truth."

Jerome
331–420

Jerome is most remembered for his Latin translation of the Bible known as the *Vulgate*. When John Wycliffe in the sixteenth century made his English translation of the Bible he used the *Vulgate* version.

Speaking about the Bible, Jerome said, "A man who is well-grounded in the testimonies of the Scripture is the bulwark of the Church...Ignorance of the Scriptures is ignorance of Christ."

John Chrysostom
c. 350–407

John Chrysostom, bishop of Constantinople, was the greatest preacher of his age and became known as "Chrysostomos," "golden-mouthed." More of his sermons still exist (over 600) than of any other Greek church father. He championed the interpretation of the Scripture in its natural meaning, and warned against the dangers of over-imaginative allegorical interpretations.

"Sacred Scripture, though, whenever it wants to teach us something like this, gives its own interpretation, and doesn't let the listener go astray. On the other hand, since the majority of listeners apply their ears to the narrative, not for the sake of gaining some profit but for enjoyment, they are at pains to take note of things able to bring enjoyment rather than those that bring profit. So, I beg you, block your ears against all distractions of that kind, and let us

follow the norm of Sacred Scripture... I exhort and entreat you all, disregard what this man and that man thinks about such things, and inquire from the Holy Scripture all these things."
John Chrysostom

Time-line of Christianity

1ST – 5TH CENTURIES	
4 BC	Birth of Christ.
AD 30	Death of Christ.
AD 30	Pentecost – when the Holy Spirit comes upon the first disciples, and the Christian church is born.
33	Stephen, the first Christian martyr, is stoned.
34	Paul persecutes the Christians but is himself converted.
49	Council at Jerusalem.
62	James, head of the Jerusalem church, martyred.
64	Rome burns; Nero blames the Christians and severe persecution follows.
70	Titus destroys Jerusalem and its temple. Separation deepens between Christianity and Judaism.
c. 150	Justin Martyr writes his First Apology, advancing Christian efforts to address competing philosophies.
155	The 86-year-old bishop Polycarp is martyred and inspires Christians to stand firm under persecution.
177	Irenaeus becomes bishop of Lyons and opposes heresies within the Church.
196	Tertullian begins his writings for which he becomes known as the "Father of Latin Theology."
205	The North African Origen begins writing and heads an important catechetical school in Alexandria.

251	Cyprian, bishop of Carthage, writes his influential book *Unity of the Church*. He is martyred in 258.
270	Antony gives away his possessions and lives as a hermit which greatly influences the development of Christian monasticism.
312	Constantine is converted to Christianity after seeing a vision of the cross and defends oppressed Christians.
325	Council of Nicea establishes the Nicene Creed
367	Athanasius' Easter Letter recognizes the New Testament canon, listing the same books as we have now in our Bibles.
387	Augustine of Hippo is converted. His writings, including the *Confessions* and *City of God* are among the most influential of all Christian books.
398	John Chrysostom, the "golden tongued" preacher is made bishop of Constantinople, from where he defends Christianity from many controversies.
405	Jerome completes the *Vulgate*, the Latin translation of the Old and New Testaments that becomes the standard Bible for the next one thousand years.
451	Council of Chalcedon affirms the doctrine of two natures in Christ.
432	Patrick goes to Ireland as a teenage slave and leads many Irish people to the Christian faith.
451	The Council of Chalcedon confirms orthodox teaching that Jesus was truly God and truly man and existed in one person.

6TH – 13TH CENTURIES

529	Benedict of Nursia establishes his monastic order. His Rule greatly influences monasticism in the West.
563	Columba goes as a missionary to Scotland where he establishes his monastic mission center at Iona.
590	Gregory becomes Pope Gregory I, known as "the Great," and influences the authority of the papacy.
664	Synod of Whitby decides that the English church will come under the authority of Rome.
716	Boniface, "Apostle of Germany," starts his missionary work on the continent of Europe.
731	The "Venerable" Bede completes his influential *Ecclesiastical History of the English Nation.*
732	The Battle of Tours, when Charles Martel rebuffs the Muslim invasion of Europe.
800	Charlemagne crowned emperor by the pope on Christmas Day.
863	The Greek brothers, Cyril and Methodius, evangelize the Serbs. Cyril invents the Cyrillic alphabet which remains the basis for the Slavonic language and is adopted in the liturgy of the Russian church.

909	The Cluny monastery is established and becomes a center for reform and expansion of monasteries. Over 1,000 Clunaic houses are founded in the following 200 years.
988	Conversion of Vladimir, Prince of Kiev, who chooses Orthodoxy to unify the Russian people.
1054	The Great Schism: the Eastern Church and Roman Church separate.
1095	The first of eventually seven crusades begins in the Holy Land at the request of Pope Urban II.
1115	Bernard founds a monastery at Clairvaux which becomes a major center of spiritual renewal.
1173	Peter Waldo founds the Waldensians, a reform movement which embraces poverty, while emphasizing preaching and teaching the Bible.
1208	St Francis of Assisi renounces wealth to follow Christ. Later he forms a group of poor friars who preach and live a simple life.
1215	The Fourth Lateran Council reaffirms Roman Catholic doctrines and strengthens the authority of the popes.
1216	Dominican monastic order founded.
1272	The last crusade ends.
1273	Thomas Aquinas completes his influential *Summa Theoligica.*

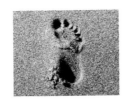

14TH – MID 17TH CENTURY

1378	Catherine of Siena goes to Rome to help heal the "Great Papal Schism" which had resulted in three popes existing at the same time. The papacy moves back to Rome from Avignon.
1382	John Wycliffe publishes the first English Bible, translated from the Vulgate.
1415	Jan Hus of Bohemia, "Daystar of the Reformation," is burned at the stake by the Council of Constance.
1456	Johann Gutenberg's press produces the first printed Bible.
1478	The Spanish Inquisition under King Ferdinand and Queen Isabella cruelly punishes all heretics.
1517	Martin Luther nails his 95 Theses to the door of the Roman Church in Wittenberg, thus starting the Protestant Reformation.
1521	Luther excommunicated.
1523	Zwingli leads the Swiss reformation from Zurich.
1525	The Anabaptist movement insists on baptism of adult believers and the separation of church and state.
1534	King Henry VIII's Act of Supremacy replaces the English monarch in place of the pope as the head of the Church of England.
1536	John Calvin publishes *The Institutes of the Christian Religion*.
1540	Ignatius Loyola founds the Jesuit order (The Society of Jesus).
1545	The Council of Trent opens. It was the Roman Catholic Church's response to Reformation theology, and it also corrected many abuses in the church.
1549	Cranmer produces the beloved Book of Common Prayer for the Church of England.
1559	John Knox leads reformation in Scotland.
1562	Pope Gregory introduces his calendar, changing the New Year from April 1 to January 1.
1572	On Saint Bartholomew's Day thousands of Protestant Huguenots are slaughtered by Catholics in France.
1609	Former Anglican preacher, John Smith, baptizes the first "Baptists."
1611	After 54 scholars had worked for four years, the Authorized or King James translation of the Bible in the English language is published.
1620	Pilgrims, fleeing persecution in Europe, arrive in America and sign the Mayflower Compact.
1633	Galileo is forced to renounce his teachings.
1646	The Westminster Confession is drafted in London.
1648	George Fox founds the Society of Friends (the Quakers).
1675	German Lutheran minister Philip Jacob Spener publishes *Pia Desideria* which becomes the "Bible" of the pietistic movement.
1678	John Bunyan's *The Pilgrim's Progress* is published and, after the Bible, becomes the best selling book in the world.
1685	Johann Sebastian Bach and George Frederick Handel born. Both give a central place to biblical themes in their compositions.
1707	Isaac Watt's *Hymns and Spiritual Songs* encourages hymn singing in churches.

MID 17TH CENTURY – MID 19TH CENTURY	
1727	Spiritual awakening at Herrnhut launches Moravian Brethren who become the forerunners of modern Protestant missionary movements.
1735	Great Awakening under the leadership of Jonathan Edwards leads to revival in American colonies.
1738	John Wesley's conversion eventually leads to the founding of the Methodist Church.
1780	Robert Raikes founds Sunday schools in which the poor and uneducated children in England are taught. Sparks the international Sunday School movement.
1793	William Carey sails to India. He organizes more Bible translations than had ever previously been produced.
1804	The British and Foreign Bible Society is founded.
1807	After William Wilberforce had spent a lifetime opposing the slave trade, the British Parliament votes to abolish it.
1811	The Campbells found the Disciples of Christ, which leads to the "Restoration Movement" of American Christianity.
1812	Adoniram and Ann Judson, the first American missionaries, sail for India and then evangelize Burma and translate the Scriptures into Burmese.
1816	Richard Allen founds the African Methodist Episcopal Church.
1817	Elizabeth Fry founds ministry to women in prison.

1830	Charles G. Finney begins his urban evangelism which greatly influences later mass evangelism in America.
1830	John Nelson Darby founds the Plymouth Brethren, a group known for its dispensational view of scriptural interpretation.
1833	John Keble's sermon, *National Apostasy*, marks the start of the Oxford Movement in England.
1854	Hudson Taylor goes to China as a missionary.
1854	Sóren Kierkegaard publishes *Attacks on Christendom*.
1854	Charles Haddon Spurgeon becomes pastor in London and later becomes most popular preacher in England.
1855	Dwight L. Moody is converted. He later becomes renowned American evangelist.
1857	David Livingstone publishes *Missionary Travels*.
1865	William Booth founds the Salvation Army.
1867	American Holiness movement is initiated by the Methodists. Later this develops into the concept that baptism in the Holy Spirit, evidenced by speaking in tongues, is a second blessing for Christians.
1870	Pope Pius IX proclaims the doctrine of Papal Infallibility.
1886	The Student Volunteer Movement encourages young people to become missionaries.
1901	Agnes Ozman is remembered as the first person of the twentieth century to experience speaking in tongues.

MID 19TH – 20TH CENTURY	
1906	Pentecostal movement starts after Asuza Street revival and is a forerunner of the modern charismatic movement.
1910-15	The "Modernist-Fundamentalist" controversy rages and exposes the great divide in American Christianity.
1914	William Durham founds the Assemblies of God. It later mushrooms into the world's largest Pentecostal denomination.
1919	Karl Barth's *Commentary on Romans* is published in which modernistic theology is criticized.
1921	First Christian radio broadcast from Pittsburgh.
1934	Cameron Townsend founds the Summer Institute of Linguistics which with Wycliffe Bible translators sets out to translate the Bible into every language group.

1945	Nazis execute Dietrich Bonhoeffer.
1948	The World Council of Churches is founded to promote Christian unity.
1949	Billy Graham's Los Angeles crusade marks the start of his international evangelism.
1950	All missionaries forced to leave China.
1960	Charismatic renewal crosses denominational boundaries and becomes a global movement.
1962	Second Vatican Council begins, bringing reforms into the Roman Catholic Church.
1963	The Baptist minister, Martin Luther King, Jr., leads a march on Washington to promote the civil rights movement.
1966-76	Despite the communistic Cultural Revolution, the Chinese church grows.

The Orthodox Church

HISTORICAL HIGHLIGHTS IN THE ORTHODOX CHURCH	
The Orthodox Church, largely ignored by both Roman Catholics and Protestants, maintains that it is the true heir of the apostolic faith of the New Testament.	
325	At the Council of Nicea St Athanasius defends the eternality of the Son of God.
589	At the Synod of Toledo the doctrine concerning the "filioque," (asserting that the Holy Spirit proceeds from the Father and the Son) is added to the Nicene Creed. This error, as Orthodox Christians view it, is later adopted by Rome.
787	The Seventh Ecumenical Council brings the centuries-old use of icons back into the Church.
988	Conversion of Russia to the Orthodox Church begins.
1054	The Great Schism. Two major doctrinal differences cause this: Rome's claim to a universal papal supremacy and her addition of the "filioque" clause to the Nicene Creed. The estrangement between the Eastern and Western churches grows into open conflict until they issue decrees of excommunication against each other. (The mutual excommunications were only lifted in 1965, as a result of a meeting of reconciliation between Pope Paul VI and Patriarch Athenogoras.)
1333	St Gregory Palamas defends the Orthodox use of the Jesus prayer: "Lord Jesus Christ, Son of God, have mercy upon me, a sinner."
1794	Missionaries arrive on Kodiak Island in Alaska; Orthodoxy introduced to North America.
1988	One thousand years of Orthodoxy in Russia.

Eastern churches

There are over 214 million Orthodox Christians today. The churches extend across Eastern Europe, Slav countries and the eastern Mediterranean.

Monasteries have played an important part in the history of the Orthodox church. Mount Athos in Greece has been the chief monastic center since the tenth century.

Icons

Veneration of icons (images used in worship) play an important part in public and private worship in the Eastern Orthodox Church. They usually depict Jesus, Mary or one of the Christian saints.

In Christian iconography, symbols are used to depict different people: the dove signifies the Holy Spirit and the fish symbolizes Jesus Christ (from the Greek ichthus, an acrostic for the name of Christ: **I**esous, **C**hristos, **T**heou, **H**uios, **S**oter [Jesus Christ, God's Son, Savior]).

The Roman Catholic Church

How do Roman Catholics view other Christian churches?

The traditional and ultra-conservative views held by Cardinal Ratzinger still hold sway in the Vatican's view of those who are outside the fold of the Roman Catholic Church.

Dominus Iesus, first published August 6, 2000 by Cardinal Ratzinger, Prefect of the Congregation for the Doctrine of the Faith, makes it clear that churches such as the Church of England (where the apostolic succession of bishops from the time of St Peter is disputed by Rome) and churches without bishops are not considered to be valid churches in the eyes of Rome.

HISTORICAL HIGHLIGHTS IN THE ROMAN CATHOLIC CHURCH	
180	Irenaeus, Bishop of Lyon, becomes the first post-Apostolic church father to assert primacy of the church in Rome over all other churches.
200	Christian ministers for the first time are called priests.
201	First specific Christian church building erected in Syria.
256	Pope Steven becomes the first head of the Roman church to openly declare succession from Peter and to hold supremacy over all church bishops.
260	First datable instance of Christians praying to the saints (Peter and Paul) for intercession.
300	Only the clergy are permitted to speak from the pulpit.
324	Constantine moves the capital to Constantinople leaving the bishop (pope) of Rome as the most powerful man in Italy.
343	The Council of Serdicia gives preference to the bishop of Rome (Pope Justin) in mediating over the Eastern churches which are embroiled in Arian heresies.

431	Council of Ephesus formally acknowledges Mary as the mother of God and that Jesus was God in the flesh.
451	Council of Chalcedon gives the same authority to the bishop of Constantinople as to the bishop of Rome; this is the beginning of the eventual schism between the Eastern and Western churches.
460	Pope Leo forbids priests to marry.
500	The word "pope," formerly applied to all church bishops, now is used solely by the bishop of Rome.
607	Pope Boniface III petitions Emperor Phocas to decree that "the See of Blessed Peter the Apostle should be the head of all the Churches" and that the title of "Universal Bishop" should be reserved exclusively for the bishop of Rome, in opposition to the bishop of Constantinople.
787	Second Council of Nicea approves of statues in churches and their veneration.
1206	St Dominic is supposedly given the rosary by the Virgin Mary.
1232	Pope Gregory IX appoints the first inquisitors.

1303	Pope Bonafice VIII issues the first papal letter to the Christian church; this is the first *de facto* use of the doctrine of Papal Infallibility, although this is not formally ratified until the 1800s.
1357	Earliest verifiable record of the Shroud of Turin.
1478	Spanish Inquisition begun by King Ferdinand and Queen Isabella
1545	Council of Trent forms to respond to the schism started by Luther, eventually ratifying a number of key doctrines which affect the Catholic church to this day. Included are: • faith alone is not sufficient for salvation • Scripture and tradition hold equal value • the seven Sacraments are necessary for salvation • transubstantiation formally acknowledged • priests forbidden to marry • Catholic canon of Scripture formally ratified.
1854	Rome establishes the Immaculate Conception dogma.
1861	Vatican Council I affirms Papal Infallibility when the Pope speaks *ex cathedra*.
1870	Papal Infallibility becomes Roman dogma.

Christian denominations

Three major divisions

Within Christianity the major division is between Orthodox and Western Christianity; and within Western Christianity the major division is between Roman Catholicism and Protestantism.

These three major church groups, Orthodox, Roman Catholic and Protestant, owe their existence to two crises in Christianity:

- the "Great Schism" between the West (Catholic) and the East (Orthodox) in 1054
- the Reformation in the sixteenth century, which led to the emergence of Protestantism.

What is the difference between a denomination and a sect?

Groupings within Christianity break down into denominations. Baptists and Lutherans are examples of Christian denominations.

Christian groups which agree with most traditional Christian teaching, but who also have some doctrine which is considered to be heretical, are called sects. Latter Day Saints (Mormons) and Jehovah's Witnesses are examples of Christian sects.

How strong are the Anglicans?

There are about 45 million Anglicans worldwide and approximately three million Episcopalians in the US.

How many Protestants are there today?

There are about 500 million Protestants.

How large is Roman Catholicism?

It is the largest of the Christian churches with approaching one billion members.

How big are the Southern Baptists?

The Southern Baptist Convention is the second largest religious body in the United States (Roman Catholics are the largest).

The Southern Baptist Convention has more churches (over 37,000) in the United States than any other religious body.

Over half of all Southern Baptists live in five Southern states: Texas, Georgia, North Carolina, Tennessee, and Alabama.

Is Christianity unique?

Is there any revelation apart from the Bible?

1. Revelation in Christ

The Bible itself teaches that God revealed himself most clearly, finally and uniquely in the person of his Son, Jesus Christ.

As the writer to the Hebrews puts it at the opening of his letter, "In the past God spoke to our forefathers through the prophets at many times and in various ways, but in these last days he has spoken to us by his Son, whom he appointed heir of all things, and through whom he made the universe." *Hebrews 1:1-2*

2. Revelation in nature

But the Bible also says that God has revealed himself in nature. "The heavens declare the glory of God; the skies proclaim the work of his hands." *Psalm 19:1*

3. Revelation as God's light

The apostle John wrote, "God is light; in him there is no darkness at all." *1 John 1:5*

Jesus said, "I am the light of the world." *John 8:12*

So when someone "sees" something that is true about God, even if he is not conscious of it, it may be said that he is catching a glimpse of Christ.

Christians, therefore, say that other religions may have partial understanding about God, but God's plan for human-kind is only possible in Christianity.

Evangelicalism

Are all religions equally valid?

The Bible teaches the view that Christianity is unique and that all the other religions of the world are not on a par with Christianity.

Jesus said, "I am the way and the truth and the life. No one comes to the Father except through me." *John 14:6*

Jesus' first followers were quite clear about this. As Peter and John were hauled up before the Sanhedrin, Peter's defense for his preaching about Jesus was, "Salvation is found in no one else, for there is no other name under heaven given to men by which we must be saved." *Acts 4:12*

Statements made by Christians about other religions and other philosophies

"Anything that one imagines of God apart from Christ is only useless thinking and vain idolatry."
Martin Luther

"The difference between Christianity and all other systems of religion consists largely in this, that in these others, men are found seeking after God, while Christianity is God seeking after men."
Thomas Arnold

"Jesus does not give recipes that show the way to God as other teachers of religion do. He is himself the way."
Karl Barth

Personal commitment

In contemporary Christianity, evangelicalism overrides denominational boundaries and refers to a number of movements within Protestantism. Each emphasizes a belief in a personal relationship with Jesus Christ and a commitment to the teaching of the Bible as the inspired word of God.

Biblical roots

The word evangelical is derived from the Greek noun *euangelion*, which is variously translated as "glad tidings," "good" or "joyful news," or "gospel." The noun *euangelion* and the verb *euangelizomai* (to announce good tidings) appear nearly one hundred times in the New Testament.

The gospel which evangelicals proclaim is defined in 1 Corinthians 15:1-4.

An historical perspective

Evangelicalism is often thought of as a contemporary phenomenon. This is a mistaken view as the evangelical spirit can be observed throughout the history of the Christian Church. The dedication, Christian commitment, disciplined lives and missionary zeal that should be characteristics of evangelicalism today were features of:
- the apostolic church
- the early church fathers
- early monasticism
- the medieval movements of reform (seen in the Cluniac, Cistercian, Franciscan and Dominican communities)

- preachers like Bernard of Clairvaux and Peter Waldo
- the forerunners to the Reformation (in such people as Wycliffe, Hus, and Savonarola).

"Evangelical" Lutherans

At the time of the Reformation, Lutherans were given the name "evangelical." They sought to steer Christianity back to the teachings of the Gospels and to renew the church by exposing it to the authoritative message of God's word.

The term "evangelical" was then used to refer to Lutheran and Reformed communions in Germany until it became almost synonymous with the term "Protestant."

Evangelical theology

Evangelicals have distinctive theological beliefs. They stress:

- the sovereignty of God – that God is a transcendent, personal, infinite Being and that he is the Creator and Sustainer of the world;
- the holiness of God – that God cannot tolerate sin, yet has love and compassion for the sinner;
- the accessibility of God – that through prayer Christians draw near to God;
- God's predeterminism – that although God's plan of redemption is predetermined by God, he allows men and women to cooperate with him and conforms their wills to his will;
- the inspiration of Scripture – it is the record of God's revelation. In matters of both faith and conduct it is the infallible, authoritative guide. It reveals that humankind is made in the image of God; that humankind is nonetheless depraved in the sense that everyone's human nature is tainted by original sin; that when Christ died on the cross he suffered God's punishment for sin (that is, he was a substitute for humankind, enabling those who trust in Christ to be united to God without being punished themselves); that Christ's death defeated the powers of darkness and meets the demands of God's justice.

Evangelicals also hold that Christ's bodily resurrection demonstrated his power over death and hell; salvation is totally by God's grace and all kinds of penance or good deeds avail nothing towards forgiveness, and new life; evangelism is incumbent on all Christians, through the proclamation of the gospel as it is found in the Bible; holiness in an individual Christian is carried on by the work of the Holy Spirit and involves confronting and overcoming evil; Christian discipleship includes caring for people's physical needs, as well as for their spiritual needs; Jesus Christ will return, visibly, and in person, to usher in his kingdom of righteousness and an everlasting new heaven and earth; and everyone will stand before God to be judged.

The charismatic movement

Charisma

The book of Acts records that on the day of Pentecost the apostles were all "filled with the Holy Spirit and began to speak in other tongues as the Spirit enabled them" (Acts 2:4). Ever since then Christians have been divided over when, how and to what extent the gifts of the Holy Spirit should be experienced by all Christians.

The word "charismatic" is derived from the Greek word *charisma* referring to a spiritual gift. Today, "charismatic" is a phrase used to refer to Christians who lay emphasis on the gifts of the Spirit. While over 20 spiritual gifts are identified in the New Testament, the ones which have attracted most attention are speaking in tongues (glossolalia), performing miracles and the gifts of healing and prophecy.

The Montanists

During the second century in western Asia Minor a group of Christians, later known as the Montanists, emphasized the importance of direct revelations by the Holy Spirit. Montanus and two women, Prisca and Maximilia, claimed the direct inspiration of the Holy Spirit and uttered prophecies while in a state of ecstatic frenzy. They claimed that they were totally possessed by the Spirit, while inaugurating a new age of revelation. Because some of their beliefs were heretical, they have often been written off as a bizarre group of enthusiasts. However, some Christians

today feel that the Christian Church has been the poorer for stamping on these positive and possibly Spirit-inspired teachings.

Revivals and Pentecostalism

Most Christian revivals, including those of the eighteenth and nineteenth centuries, have included unusual manifestations of what was purported to be the work of the Holy Spirit.

Pentecostal churches believe in the "Four-Square Gospel." Its four cornerstones are:

- personal salvation through faith in Jesus Christ,
- divine healing,
- second coming of Christ, and
- Spirit baptism with evidence of tongues.

USA

Through the work of evangelist Oral Roberts and California dairy farmer Demos Shakarian (who founded the Full Gospel Business Men's Fellowship International in 1951) Pentecostalism started to come to the forefront in the United States. The South African-born David J. du Plessis (1905–87), sometimes called "Mr Pentecost," made it into an international movement.

Protestants and Roman Catholics

In the 1950s a significant number of individuals in many of the Protestant churches experienced spiritual crises leading to overwhelming experiences of spiritual renewal which they called "the baptism of the Holy Spirit." By the early 1960s this movement grew rapidly and evolved into what became known as "charismatic renewal." The first meeting of charismatics from non-Pentecostal traditions was organized by du Plessis in 1962.

By 1967 the renewal movement had spread to the Roman Catholic Church where its most outspoken supporter was the Belgian Cardinal Joseph Suenens.

Throughout the 1970s and 1980s it spread like wildfire through the American churches until all the larger denominations had charismatic renewal groups.

The charismatic movement became further popularized through the television ministries of several leading charismatics such as Rex Humbard, Marion "Pat" Robertson, Paul Crouch, and James Robinson.

A global phenomena

Leaping over all geographic and denominational boundaries the charismatic movement spread to Protestant and Roman Catholic churches throughout the world.

Korea

One spectacular example of the power of the Spirit was seen in Korea in the ministry of an Assemblies of God pastor in Seoul, David (Paul) Yonggi Cho. In 1958 he started a tent church which mushroomed into the world's largest congregation, the Yoido Full Gospel Church, boasting a membership of more than half a million.

Britain

In Britain the movement was supported by the publications and conferences spearheaded by the Fountain Trust which was established in 1964.

South America

The charismatic movement renewed thousands of individual churches throughout Latin America, both Roman Catholic and Protestant. One estimate reckoned that by 1987 between 80 and 85% of Protestants were Pentecostals or charismatics.

WHO WERE THE WELL KNOWN CHRISTIANS IN THE TWENTIETH CENTURY?

Billy Graham, evangelist

C. S. Lewis, writer

Mother Teresa, ministry among the poor, destitute and dying of Calcutta

Karl Barth, theologian

Alexander Solzhenitsyn, novelist

Martin Luther King, Jr., campaigner for social justice

Jimmy Carter, 39th president of the United States

2 *ISLAM*

CONTENTS	
	page

Introduction

Defining Islam

Islam is a monotheistic religion which is characterized by

- the acceptance of the doctrine of submission to God and
- Mohammed as the chief and last prophet of God.

Islam is on the ascendancy; the spread of the Muslim faith appears to be unstoppable. By the year 2010 it is expected to be the largest religion in the world.

Terrorism and Islam

Most Muslims do not support terrorism and have denounced the atrocities of September 11, 2001. They point out that the Prophet Muhammad once said after a battle: "We are going from the lesser *jihad* to the greater *jihad*," meaning that the challenge of living one's daily life is the greater struggle. They emphasize that *jihad* has intellectual, spiritual and moral dimensions.

Nevertheless, in 1998 Osama bin Laden, who always claimed to be a devout Muslim, called for all Americans and Jews, including children, to be killed. He continued to call for the destruction of the US, Israel, and the Saudi monarchy, stating that with these obstacles removed, Islam's three holiest sites, Mecca, Medina and Jerusalem, will be liberated.

On November 1st, 2001, British Prime Minister, Tony Blair, declared that there is "a gulf of misunderstanding between the Arab and Muslim world and the West."

We can attempt to bridge this gulf by paying attention to what Islam really teaches.

Origin of Islam

Only one God

In the sixth century CE, in Mecca (Makkah), Saudi Arabia (then western Arabia), the Prophet Muhammad began to preach the message of Islam, that there is only one God.

Names
Islam

The Arabic meaning of the word "Islam" is "submission."

The word comes from the same root as the Arabic word *salam* (and the Hebrew *shalom*), which means "peace." The religion of Islam teaches that in order to achieve true peace of mind one must submit to God and live according to his divinely revealed law.

Muslim

A Muslim is a follower of Islam.

The word "Muslim" with a capital "M" denotes someone who follows the religion of Muhammad.

The word "muslim" with a small "m" is someone who submits to God's will.

Muhammad

The name of the founder of Islam. (Muslims object to being called Muhammadans, as Muhammad is not worshiped in the way Christ is worshiped by Christians.)

Allah

Allah (the Arabic word for God) is the Supreme Being, the one and only God.

Muslim beliefs

Muslims believe that Muhammad was the last of a line of prophets who revealed Allah's will to the world.

They submit to, that is, obey, the will of Allah as revealed in the teachings of Muhammad and seek to live lives that please Allah.

A taste of the Qur'an (Koran)
Compulsion in religion

"There shall be no compulsion in religion." Qur'an 2:263

The fate of unbelievers

"As for the unbelievers, it is the same whether or not you forewarn them; they will not have faith. God has set a seal upon their hearts and ears; their sight is dimmed and grievous punishment awaits them." Qur'an 2:2-6

"He that chooses a religion over Islam, it will not be accepted from him and in the world to come he will be one of the lost." Qur'an 3:86

"God's curse be upon the infidels! Evil is that for which they have bartered away their souls. To deny God's own revelation, grudging that he should reveal his bounty to whom he chooses from among his servants! They have incurred God's most inexorable wrath. An ignominious punishment awaits the unbelievers." Qur'an 2:92-6

Islam the only way to God

"The only true faith in God's sight is Islam." Qur'an 3:19

Fighting for the faith

"Fight for the sake of God those that fight against you, but do not attack them first. God does not love the aggressors. Slay them wherever you find them. Drive them out of the places from which they drove you. Idolatry is worse than carnage." Qur'an 2:190-3

Allah and light

"Allah is the light of the heavens and the earth. His light may be compared to a niche that enshrines a lamp, the lamp within a crystal of star-like brilliance. It is lit from a blessed olive tree neither eastern nor western. Its very oil would almost shine forth, though no fire touched it. Light upon light; Allah guides to His light whom He will." Qur'an 24:34

Allah created you

"It was He who created you from dust, making you a little germ, and then a clot of blood. He brings you infants into the world; you reach manhood, then decline into old age (though some of you die young), so that you may complete your appointed term and grow in wisdom." Qur'an 40:67

Muhammad: Islam's founder

An historical figure

Unlike the founders of many religions, Muhammad is an historical figure whose life is well documented.

Muhammad was born in 570 CE at Mecca in Arabia. His father, Abdullah, a poor merchant, was a member of the powerful Quaraysh tribe, but died before Muhammad was born. His mother died when he was six. Muhammad was then brought up by his uncle Abu Talib. He became a merchant, well known for his honesty. He was called "Al-Amen," the Trustworthy. He married a wealthy widow, Khadijah, who was 15 years older than him. He became concerned

about the poverty and inequalities of life in Mecca and also about its superstition and polytheism. From Jews and Christians in the area he learned about the teaching of the Bible and of Jesus Christ. He often went to a cave near Mecca to meditate.

Muhammad's mission

At the age of 40 Muhammad was called by Allah to be his prophet. His first biographer, Muhammad Ibn Ishaq, captures the moment: "While I was asleep an angel came to me with something to read and said, 'Read this.' I replied, 'I cannot read.' Then he pressed the material against me so firmly that I thought I would die, and said again, 'Read it.' The angel repeated this instruction for a third time, so I replied, 'What should I read?' The angel said:

> 'Read in the name of the Lord your
> God.
> He who created man from an embryo.
> Read, for the Lord your God is
> merciful, like no one else on earth.
> He who instructed men by the pen
> He taught him what he never knew.'

FACTFILE ON MUHAMMAD	
c. 570 CE	Born in Mecca, on the Arabian peninsula.
c. 595 CE	Marries Khadija, a wealthy widow, but becomes dissatisfied with the luxury that surrounds him. Starts to meditate.
c. 610 CE	On Mount Hira the angel Gabriel appears to him, revealing that he is to be God's messenger.
c. 613 CE	He becomes a preacher, telling the people of Mecca to reject their idols and worship Allah.
622 CE	Forced to flee from Mecca, he travels to Medina.
629 CE	Returns to Mecca with many followers and is warmly welcomed.
632 CE	Dies in Medina.

"When I woke up it was as if these words had been written on my heart."

Muhammad's mission was to teach that "there is nothing divine or worthy of being worshiped except for Almighty God."

Hijrah

At the time of Muhammad's birth most people in Arabia believed in many different gods and idolatry was common. In this polytheistic world, Muhammad's message about "only One God" soon aroused great opposition especially from Muhammad's own tribe which guarded the Ka'aba, a sanctuary dedicated to many gods. This sanctuary later became the House of Allah and the center of Islamic pilgrimage.

In 622 Muhammad and his followers were thrown out of Mecca by Meccan merchants and forced to flee to Yathrib (later called Medina), 300 miles to the north. Muhammad's journey to Medina, known as *Hijrah*, marks the dawn of the Muslim era and the Muslim calendar dates from this year.

Medina

He transformed his followers from a religious group into a powerful political force. He proclaimed war against infidels as a religious duty, and his armed religious convoys spread his teaching throughout Arab countries. In 629, hearing that his own tribe was plotting to kill him, he marched against Mecca with an army of 10,000 Muslims and took the city. By the following year he had taken control of almost all Arabia.

Muhammad smashed the 350 idols of the Ka'aba and then made it the pilgrimage center for Islam. By his death in 632 he had over 100,000 followers and had shaped the Arab world for centuries to come.

The four caliphs

Caliph is an arabic word meaning successor or deputy. After Muhammad died the Muslim world faced a crisis which threatened its very existence – who would now lead the new community?

The first caliph: Abu Bakr

Abu Bakr, the first caliph, consolidated the power of the infant Islamic state after the Prophet's unexpected death.

The second caliph: Omar

Under the second caliph, Omar, the Arabs found themselves with an empire and enormous wealth which was used to create the first welfare state in human history.

The third caliph: Uthman

Under caliph Uthman the Qur'an was compiled, copied, and disseminated.

The fourth caliph: Ali

Caliph Ali, the last of the Prophet's friends to hold the office of caliph, spent the next five years fighting a bitter civil war which saved the infant Muslim state.

Time-line: 570–1517 CE

TIME-LINE: 570–1517 CE	
c. 570	Muhammad born in Mecca.
632	Death of Muhammad.
654	Islam spreads into all of North Africa.
718	Islam now rules all of the Persian Empire and most of the old Roman world (the Middle East, North Africa and Spain).
Early 1300s	Islam becomes the official religion of the Ottoman Empire.
1517	Sultan of Ottoman Empire becomes caliph.

POTTED HISTORY OF ISLAM	
c. 570	Muhammad born in Mecca.
632	Death of Muhammad. His father-in-law, Abu-Bakr, becomes the first caliph.
637	The Arabs occupy the Persian capital of Ctesiphon.
638	The Romans are defeated at the Battle of Yarmouk and the Muslims enter Palestine.
641	Islam spreads into Egypt.
654	Islam spreads into all of North Africa.
661	Damascus replaces Medina as the seat of the caliphate. The Umayyad family rules Islam until 750.
662	Egypt falls under the control of the Umayyad and Abbasid caliphates until 868.
669	The Muslim conquest reaches Morocco in North Africa.
700	Islamic mysticism (Sufism) becomes prominent.
710	Tariq ibn Malik with a group of Muslims enters Spain.
711	7,000 Muslims invade Gibraltar.
718	Nearly all of the Iberian Peninsula comes under Islamic control. Islam now rules all of the Persian Empire and most of the old Roman world.

During the seventeenth century, under the powerful Mogul emperors, most of the subcontinent of India was under Islamic control.

During the seventeenth and eighteenth centuries Muslim traders took the teaching of Muhammad from India to Malaysia, Indonesia, the Philippines and eastern China.

During the nineteenth century the Islamic faith spread to Libya, West Africa and the Sudan. Today, Islam is the official religion of approximately 45 countries.

750	The Abbasids take over the rule of the Islamic world (except for Spain).
768	First biography of Muhammad is written by Muhammad Ibn Ishaq.
766–809	Caliph Harun al-Raschid. A major figure in the Arabian Nights, he rules until 809.
c. 800 –850	al-Khwarizmi, scholar, astronomer, mathematician. Latin translations of his works in medieval Europe make known the Arabic system of numbers. The word algebra comes from the title of one of his books.
10th century	Rhazes, the greatest physician of medieval times, discovers the difference between measles and smallpox.
945	Shiites invade Baghdad. Until the sixteenth century, rule of Islamic civilization is decentralized and different sects are ruled by different rulers.
870–960	Mohammad al-Farabi, the greatest of the *faylasufs* (philosophers). He teaches that the enlightened individual can perfect his life through philosophy. The ninth to the eleventh centuries are the greatest period of Muslim thought and culture.
997	Mahmud, ruler of a Turkish dynasty in Gujarat and known as the "Sword of Islam," conducts 17 raids into north-western India.

980–1037	Avicenna, philosopher and physician. He discovers that disease can be spread through the contamination of water and that tuberculosis is contagious. His medical book, the *Canon of Medicina* is accepted as authoritative for the next 600 years.
1100	Islamic rule is weakened as the result of power struggles among Islamic leaders and the Christian crusades.
c. 1050 –1122	Omar Khayyam, born in Persia, poet, mathematician, astronomer. Possible author of renowned poem *The Rubaiyat* (a poetry anthology).
1248	Muslim control of Spain is reduced to the kingdom of Granada, which survives for a further two centuries.
Early 1300s	Islam becomes the official religion of the Ottoman Empire.
1453	The Ottomans defeat the Byzantine Empire and continue expanding into the Balkans. The Ottoman Turkish Empire moves its capital from Bursa to Istanbul (Constantinople).
1492	Ferdinand of Aragon and Isabella of Castile, later benefactors of Christopher Columbus, end Muslim rule in Spain.
1517	Selim I, Sultan of the Ottoman Empire becomes caliph, the temporal and spiritual leader of the Muslim world.

The Qur'an

The Qur'ran
What is it?
The Qur'an (Koran) is Islam's holy book containing its fundamental beliefs.

What does it mean?
The Arabic word Al-Qur'an literally means "the recitation." When used in connection with Islam, the word Qur'an means God's final message to humankind that was revealed to the Prophet Muhammad.

How did it come into existence?
Muslims believe that it has always existed in heaven where it was written in Arabic on a tablet of stone. It contains the words of Allah as they were spoken to Muhammad over a period of 23 years. It has not been altered in any way since it was first written by Muhammad's scribes

What subjects does it cover?
It teaches the Straight Path through life and includes teaching about:

- worship
- how to treat other people
- how to lead a good life
- what clothes to wear
- what food to eat.

Learning the Qur'an
Muslims are devoted to the teachings of the Qur'an and even if they cannot speak Arabic, most Muslims will still try to read the Qur'an in its original language.

Many Muslims memorize the whole of the Qur'an in Arabic. Such Muslims are given the title *Hafiz*.

The authority of the Qur'an
The Qur'an is the final, direct revelation from God, and is therefore the ultimate source of authority and the main source for the *Shari'ah*, the Islamic Law.

Shari'ah is the totality of God's prescriptions for humankind, encompassing all aspects of life with no separation between religious and secular subjects.

The Qur'an describes itself as a "preserved tablet" (85:22), as it was pre-existent in heaven.

Translations of the Qur'an
The only authoritative text of the Qur'an is the original Arabic. Muslims regard "translations" of the Qur'an into other languages as paraphrases of the original.

Infallible
For Muslims the *Qur'an* is infallible in the sense that it is the final source of authority in all matters of belief and behavior and law and it contains no errors and is complete and unchanging.

The literal word of God
The *Qur'an* claims that it is the literal word of God.

Unlike the sacred scriptures of other religions, the Qur'an has been perfectly preserved in both its words and meaning in a living language. It is seen as a living

miracle in the Arabic language, inimitable in its style, form and spiritual impact.

The Qur'an, in contrast to many other religious books, did not become authoritative as a result of a decree issued by a religious council many years after it was written, but was always thought to be the word of God.

Opening the Qur'an

The Qur'an is about the same length as the New Testament and has 114 chapters (surahs) each of which has a name as well as a number. The contents of the Qur'an are not arranged according to subject matter and are not in any chronological order. Rather, they are arranged according to length, with the shortest surah at the end and the longest toward the beginning.

The opening *surah*, called *al Fatihah*, ("The Opener") is a prayer asking Allah for guidance. It is a favorite prayer of Muslims.

"Praise be to God, the Lord of the worlds!
The compassionate, the merciful!
King of the day of judgment!
Thee only do we worship, and to thee do we cry for help.
Guide us on the straight path,
The path of those to whom you have been gracious –
With whom you are not angry, and who do not go astray."

Every *surah*, except for the ninth one, begins, "*Bismillah al rahman, al rahime,*" "In the name of Allah the Compassionate, the Merciful."

The *Hadith*

The *Hadith* ("saying") are the traditional sayings and actions of Muhammad which are not found in the Qur'an. Though not as important as the Qur'an itself, they have become an authoritative basis for Islamic law and are still followed by Muslims today.

The Five Pillars of Islam

The Five Pillars of Islam

Muslims throughout the world have the same basic beliefs, which are summed up in the "five pillars" of Islam. A Muslim is taught that anyone who dies observing them will enter heaven:

- *shahada:* confession of faith
- *salat:* ritual prayer
- *zakat:* giving money to the poor
- *saum:* fasting during Ramadan
- *hajj:* going on pilgrimage to Mecca.

Shahada

The first pillar is a statement of faith:

- "There is no God but Allah."
- "Mohammed is the prophet/messenger of Allah."

These statements are recited by new converts when they become Muslims.

Muslims believe that there is no entity worthy of worship except Allah alone and that Muhammad (often called *pbuh*) was his messenger. The first pillar establishes that God Almighty alone must be obeyed.

Salat

Salat consists of prayer, conducted five times a day, kneeling on a prayer mat and facing the *Ka'aba* in Mecca.

The public call to prayer (*adhan*) is sounded by a *muezzin* ("caller," a Muslim crier) from a minaret – a tower which is a part of the mosque. This prayer has seven statements:

1. Allah is most great. (Four times)

2. I testify that there is no god but Allah. (Twice)
3. I testify that Muhammad is the Messenger of Allah. (Twice)
4. Come to prayer. (Twice)
5. Come to salvation. (Twice) (During the morning call to prayer, the statement, "Prayer is better than sleep," is inserted here.)
6. Allah is most great. (Twice)
7. There is no god but Allah. (Twice)

The five times when prayer must be observed are:

- on rising
- at noon
- in mid-afternoon
- after sunset
- before retiring.

Prescribed prayers, the first surah (chapter) and other sections from the Qur'an, must all be recited in Arabic.

The *Hadith* (book of tradition) stipulates the following postures during this time of prayer: standing, bowing, kneeling, hands, foreheads and noses touching the floor and, finally, sitting back on one's heels. The Qur'an says "perform the prayer," and through these postures Muslims indicate their submission to God.

Zakat

Giving alms (money) to the poor and needy is the third pillar. All Muslims are required to give one fortieth (2.5%) of their income to charity every year.

Saum

Muslims fast from dawn to sundown each day during the holy month of Ramadan. No food or drink may be consumed during the daylight hours; no smoking or sexual pleasures may be enjoyed. Many Muslims eat two meals a day during Ramadan, one before sunrise and one shortly after sunset.

Hajj

Muslims are commanded to make a pilgrimage to Mecca at least once in their lives, preferably in person, although it can be done by proxy. This pilgrimage is an essential part of a Muslim's salvation. It involves a set of ceremonies and rituals lasting for six days, many of which center around the *Ka'aba* (the House of Allah) shrine in Mecca.

Jihad

A sixth religious duty is often associated with the five pillars. This is the *jihad*. A traditional view of *jihad* states that when the situation warrants, men are required to go to war to spread Islam or defend it against infidels.

One who dies in a *jihad* is guaranteed eternal life in Paradise (heaven) and is considered a *Shahid*, a martyr for Islam.

A better interpretation of *jihad* is striving in the way of Allah by pen, tongue, hand, media and, if inevitable, with weapons. However, *jihad* does not include striving for individual or national power, dominance, glory, wealth, prestige or pride.

ENTERING PARADISE

Mu'ad ibn Jabal said: "I said to Allah's Messenger (peace be upon him): Inform me about an act which would entitle me to enter into Paradise, and distance me from the Hell-Fire."

He (the Prophet) said: "You have asked me about a matter [which ostensibly appears to be] difficult but it is easy for those for whom Allah, the Exalted, has made it easy. Worship Allah and do not associate anything with him, establish prayer, pay the Zakat, observe the fast of Ramadhan and perform Hajj to the House (Ka'aba)."
Prophet Muhammad

Holy war

This word *jihad* is often said to mean holy war. But the term "holy war" was coined in Europe during the crusades, and refers to the war against Muslims. The phrase does not have a counterpart in Islamic glossary, and *jihad* is certainly not its translation.

Striving

In the Qur'an and *Hadith*, *jihad* is derived from the root *jhd* the primary meaning of which is to strive or to exert oneself. In its primary sense *jihad* is an inner act, a fight to eradicate one's own evil actions and inclinations.

The translation of *jihad* into "holy war," combined with the false idea that Islam is the "religion of the sword," has resulted in the eclipsing of the spiritual meaning of the word.

Is jihad *a holy war against Jews and Christians?*

A defense

The word, *jihad*, came to mean the defence of *dar al-islam*, that is, the Islamic world, from any invasion by non-Islamic forces. The earliest wars of Islamic history, which threatened the very existence of Islam, were known as *jihad* in this outward sense of "holy war."

But on returning from one of these early wars the Prophet Muhammad said to his followers that they had returned from the lesser holy war to the greater holy war. The greater *jihad* is the inner battle against everything that prevents Muslims from living in obedience to Allah.

Jihad and the pillars of Islam

Although *jihad* is not one of the "pillars of Islam," it is a part of all of the "pillars." From the spiritual point of view, all of the "pillars" should be viewed in the light of an inner *jihad*.

Jihad and *shahada* (confession of faith)

The fundamental witnesses, "There is no

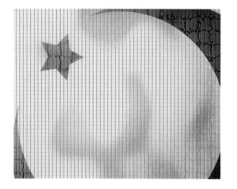

divinity but Allah" and "Muhammad is the Messenger of Allah," through the utterance of which a person becomes a Muslim, are not only statements about the truth but the weapons for the practice of inner *jihad*.

Jihad and *salat* (ritual prayer)

The daily prayers (*salat*) are also a never-ending *jihad*, since to perform the prayers with regularity necessitates the exertion of the will and an unending battle against forgetfulness, dissipation and laziness.

Jihad and *zakat* (giving money to the poor)

The giving of *zakat* is a form of *jihad*. To become detached from one's own wealth demands great effort in the fight against the coveteousness and greed which lives in everyone. Through the payment of *zakat* social justice is being established.

Jihad and *saum* (fasting during Ramadan)

During the fast of Ramadan Muslims wear the armor of inner purity and detachment against the passions and temptations of the world.

Jihad and *hajj* (going on pilgrimage to Mecca)

The *hajj* to Mecca is impossible without long preparation, which often includes suffering and endurance. It should include great exertion. Hence the Prophet Muhammad said, "The *hajj* is the most excellent of all *jihads*."

More Islamic beliefs

Angels

The existence of angels is important to
Islamic teaching. Gabriel, the leading
angel, appeared to Mohammad and gave
him the revelations in the Qur'an. Islam
teaches that:

- Allah created angels and they are his
  servants and messengers;
- angels communicate God's messages
  to his prophets;
- angels strengthen everything that is
  good in a person;
- everyone has at least one angel.

Satan

Shaytan is the devil, an angel who
disobeyed Allah, and tempts Muslims to
disobey the teaching of the Qur'an.

Prophets

In Islam God has spoken through
numerous prophets down through the
centuries.

The six greatest are:

- Adam
- Noah
- Abraham
- Moses
- Jesus
- Mohammad.

Mohammad, the last and greatest of
God's prophets, is so esteemed by
Muslims that after saying his name they
usually say the blessing, "peace be upon
him." The name Mohammad is often
abbreviated to "*pbuh.*"

Judgment day

The last day will be a time of resurrection and judgment. Those who follow and obey Allah and Mohammad pass over the narrow *Assirat Bridge* to heaven, called *Jannah* (Paradise), a place of pleasure with beautiful gardens. Those who oppose Allah fall off the bridge into hell (*jahannam*) where they suffer physically and experience "fire in their hearts."

> "The Trumpet shall be sounded and all who are in heaven and earth shall fall down fainting, except those that shall be spared by Allah. Then the Trumpet will sound again and they shall rise and gaze around them. The earth will shine with the light of her Lord, and the Book will be laid open. The prophets and witnesses shall be brought in and all shall be judged with fairness: none shall be wronged. Every soul shall be paid back according to its deeds, for Allah knows of all their actions."
> *Qur'an 39:68*

Jesus

Islam regards Jesus as one of the prophets of the Islamic faith, but not as the Son of God.

> "The Messiah, Jesus Son of Mary, was only a messenger of God."
> *Qur'an 4:157-158*
> "They do blaspheme who say: 'God is Christ the son of Mary.'" *Qur'an 112:1*

Salat

The ritual prayer, in Arabic *salat*, means supplication and is derived from the word "silah" which means link. The prayer is a link between the human being and his Lord and is full of supplication to the Lord from its beginning to its end.

Salat provides a chance of direct communion with the Creator five times a day wherein man renews his covenant with God – again and again seeking guidance. "You alone we worship and to you alone we turn for help. Guide us to the straight path." (1:5,6)

Punishment for adultery

The official punishment for adultery is 100 lashes, although this varies from country to country.

> "The adulterer and the adulteress, scourge each one of them with a hundred stripes. And let no pity for them stop you from obeying Allah. And let a party of believers witness their punishment." *Qur'an 24:2.6*

Eating and drinking

Muslims are not allowed to eat pork or to drink alcohol. They are taught that the devil is in every grape.

Unity

Mohammad said in his last sermon: "Every Muslim is a brother to every other Muslim. You are in a great brotherhood."

Belief about God

God

- The oneness of God (*tawhid*). The absolute unity of God is the cardinal principal of Islam.
- The name of the one true God is Allah.
- Allah is all-knowing.
- Allah is all-powerful and the sovereign judge.
- Allah is beyond human understanding.
- Allah created all things.
- Allah is merciful and compassionate.
- Allah has always existed and will always exist, and is not affected by time.
- Allah is present with Muslims all the time.
- Muhammad (*pbuh*) is the messenger of God.
- God has 99 names.

Not a personal God

Allah is not an interacting, personal God. He is so far above humans in every way that he cannot be experienced in a personal relationship.

> "He is Allah, the One. Allah is eternal and Absolute. None is born of him. He is Unborn. There is none like unto him." *Qur'an 112*

Attempting to define God

In the Qur'an God describes himself in many places and in many ways.

> "Allah is close." *Qur'an 2:186*

> "When my servants ask thee concerning me, I am indeed close (to them): I listen to the prayer of every suppliant when he calleth on me: Let them also, with a will, listen to my call, and believe in me: That they may walk in the right way. Allah is loving and forgiving." *Qur'an 11:90*

> "But ask forgiveness of your Lord, and turn unto him (in repentance): For my Lord is indeed full of mercy and loving-kindness." *Qur'an 1:2*

> "Praise be to God, the Cherisher and Sustainer of the worlds. Allah is all-knowing and caring." *Qur'an 2:268*

> "And your God is One God: There is no god but He, Most Gracious, Most Merciful." *Qur'an 5:72*

> "Say: He is God, the One and Only; God, the Eternal, Absolute; He begetteth not, nor is He begotten; And there is none like unto Him." *Qur'an 19:35*

Many names for God

Muslims are taught that Allah Almighty has scores of names, the most well-known among them being "Allah." These names, which are found throughout the Qur'an, embody the major characteristics of Allah Almighty such as "The Gracious," "The Merciful," "The Majestic," "The Supreme."

> "Allah! There is no god save him. His are the most beautiful names." *Qur'an, 20:8*

"He is Allah, other than whom there is no other god, He is the 'Knower' of (all things) both the unseen and the seen; He is the 'Gracious' the 'Merciful'. He is Allah, other than whom there is no god, the 'Sovereign,' the 'Holy One,' the (source of) 'Peace,' the 'Guardian of Faith,' the 'Overseer,' the 'Majestic,' the 'Irresistible,' the 'Supreme': Glory be to Allah! (highly exalted is he) above the partners they attribute to him. He is Allah the 'Creator,' the 'Innovator,' the 'Fashioner'. His are the Most Beautiful Names: Whatever is in the heavens and on earth do glorify Him: and He is the 'Mighty.' the 'Wise.'" *Qur'an, 59:20-24*

As well as many names for Allah, the Qur'an contains many descriptions of Allah.

"God! There is no god but he, – the living, the self-subsisting, eternal. No slumber can seize him nor sleep.
"His are all things in the heavens and on earth. Who is there can intercede in his presence except as he permitteth?
He knoweth what (appeareth to his creatures as) before or after or behind them. Nor shall they compass aught of his knowledge except as he willeth. His throne doth extend over the heavens and the earth, and he feeleth no fatigue in guarding and preserving them for he is the most high the supreme in glory." *Qur'an 2:255*

The 99 names of God

"THE NINETY-NINE BEAUTIFUL NAMES"

The 99 names of God describe his qualities but not his essence (Surah 59). They are called "The Ninety-Nine Beautiful Names," or "Attributes of Perfection."

These are memorized and are used in meditation and when they wish to praise Allah or call on him for guidance or help.

A list of the 99 Names of God (Asma-ullah) which are given in the Qur'an and Hadith:

Arabic - English

1. Allah (jallah jalaluh) - God (in all His Majesty)
2. ar-Rahman - the All-Merciful
3. ar-Rahim - the All-Compassionate
4. al-Malik - the King
5. al-Quddus - the All-Holy
6. as-Salam - Peace, Source of Peace
7. al-Mumin - the All-Faithful
8. al-Muhaymin - the Guardian of Faith and Preserver of Safety
9. al-Aziz - the Almighty, the Hard of Access
10. al-Jabbar - the Irresistible
11. al-Mutakabbir - the Great, the Grand
12. al-Khaliq - the Creator
13. al-Bari - the Maker
14. al-Musawwir - the Fashioner of Forms
15. al-Ghaffar - the Ever-Forgiving
16. al-Qahhar - the All-Compelling
17. al-Wahhab - the Ever-Giving
18. al-Razzaq - the Ever-Providing
19. al-Fattah - the Opener (of the heart), the Victory-Giver
20. al-Alim - the All-Knowing, the Omniscient
21. al-Qabid - the Straitener
22. al-Basit - the Expansive, the Munificent
23. al-Khafid - the Abaser
24. al-Rafic - the Exalter
25. al-Mu'izz - the Honorer
26. al-Mudhill - the Humiliator, the Degrader
27. az-Sami'eh - the All-Hearing
28. al-Basir - the All-Seeing
29. al-Hakam - the Arbitrator
30. al-Adl - Justice, the Just
31. al-Latif - the Subtle, the All-Pervading, the Gentle
32. al-Khabir - the Informed, the All-Aware
33. al-Halim - the Forbearing, the Indulgent
34. al-Azim - the Tremendous, the Infinite
35. al-Ghafur - the Totally Forgiving
36. ash-Shakur - the Grateful, the Appreciative
37. al-Ali - the All-High
38. al-Kabir - the Great
39. al-Hafiz - the Safeguard
40. al-Muqit - the Nourisher
41. al-Hasib - the All-Calculating
42. al-Jalil - the Majestic
43. al-Karim - the Generous
44. ar-Raqib - the Watchful
45. al-Mujib - the Answerer
46. al-Wasic - the All-Encompassing

47.	al-Hakim - the Wise		73.	al-Awwal - the First
48.	al-Wadud - the Loving, the Kind One		74.	al-Akhir - the Last
49.	al-Majid - the All-Glorious		75.	as-Zahir - the Outward, the Manifest
50.	al-Bacith - the Raiser of the Dead		76.	al-Batin - the Inward, the Hidden
51.	ash-Shahid - the Witness		77.	al-Waali - the Ruler
52.	al-Haqq - the Truth, the Real, the Absolute		78.	al-Mutacali - the Transcendent
53.	al-Wakil - the Dependable		79.	al-Barr v - the Good, the Beneficent
54.	al-Qawiy - the Strong		80.	al-Tawwab - the Ever-Returning, the Ever-Relenting
55.	al-Matin - the Steadfast		81.	al-Muntaqim - the Avenger
56.	al-Waliy - the Patron, the Helper		82.	al-Afuw - the Effacer of Sins
57.	al-Hamid - the All-Praiseworthy		83.	ar-Raúf - the All-Pitying
58.	al-Muhsi - the Accounter, the Numberer		84.	Maliku-l-Mulk - the King of the Kingdom
59.	al-Mubdic - the Initiator		85.	Dhu-Jalali wal-ikram - the Possessor of Majesty and Generosity
60.	al-Mucid - the Reinstater, the Bringer-Back		86.	al-Muqsit - the Equitable, the Requiter
61.	al-Muhyi - the Life-Giver		87.	al-Jamic - the Unifier, the Gatherer
62.	al-Mumit - the Bringer of Death		88.	al-Ghani - the All-Rich, the Independent
63.	al-Hayy - the Ever-Living		89.	al-Mughni - the Enricher, the Emancipator
64.	al-Qayyum - the Ever-Self-Sustaining		90.	al-Mani'eh - the Shielder, the Defender
65.	al-Wajid - the Finder, the Unfailing		91.	ad-Darr - the Harmer
66.	al-Majid - the Magnificent		92.	an-Nafi'eh - the Benefactor
67.	al-Wahid - the Single, the All-Inclusive, the Indivisible		93.	an-Nurthe - Light
68.	as-Samad - the Self-Sufficient, the Impregnable		94.	al-Hadithe - Guide
69.	al-Qadir - the All-Able		95.	al-Badi'eh - the Peerless, the Originator
70.	al-Muqtadir - the All-Determiner		96.	al-Baqic - the Immutable, the Eternal
71.	al-Muqaddim - the Promoter, He who brings forward		97.	al-Warith - the Inheritor
72.	al-Muakhkhir - the Delayer, He who puts far away		98.	ar-Rashid - the Infallible Teacher and Knower
			99.	as-Sabur - the Patient, the Timeless

Worship

Mosques

The first Muslim mosque, built by
Muhammad in Medina, had wooden
walls and a thatch of palm leaves for its
roof. A simple mosque was built over
the place where Muhammad died. Today
Islamic mosques are among the world's
most impressive buildings.

Layout of a mosque

Muslims can and do pray anywhere. But
on Fridays, at noon, all Muslim men,
and women if they wish, are expected to
attend their house of prayer.

Mosques have a tall minaret from
which the call to prayer is made. Their
spacious courtyards (*sahn*) are
surrounded by shady arcades (*riwags*).
Fountains (*fauwara*) in the courtyard
symbolize purity and are used by
worshipers to bathe their hands,
forearms and legs below the knee. This
ablution (*wudu*) takes place before
prayer and points to the need for inner
purity.

Inside is the prayer hall (*zulla*) where
the worshipers meet. They must face
Mecca to pray and an empty arch
(*mihrah*) built in one of the walls
indicates the direction of Mecca. Next to
the *mihrah* is the *minbar* (pulpit) from
where the *imam* (prayer-leader) leads the
prayers and preaches.

Islam does not allow human figures to
be shown. Islamic buildings are often
decorated with intricate and very
beautiful geometric shapes and patterns.

Ramadan

The holy month of *Ramadan* is the most
important of the festivals as it
commemorates the time when
Muhammad received his first revelation
from Allah.

Fasting in *Ramadan*

Muslims fast throughout the month-long *Ramadan*. They do not, however, fast as an ascetic practice but to:

- discipline themselves
- remember the world's poor
- focus on Allah's blessings.

Id ul-Fitr

When the new moon is seen, the fast of *Ramadan* ends with the festival of *Id al-fitr*. This involves a visit to the mosque and a feast of special foods.

Times of life

Muslims engage in special ceremonies and prayers at every stage of life.

Birth

No sooner is a baby born than a prayer is whispered into his/her ear.

Naming

A naming ceremony (*aqiqah*) follows seven days after birth.

Marriage

The Qur'an teaches that marriage is a gift from God and is beneficial because it acts as a "cement" in society and regulates sexual relationships and secures family life.

They are encouraged to marry only Muslims.

Death

Muslims are not cremated since they believe that dead bodies must not be harmed but respected. A dead person is always buried with the head toward Mecca.

ISLAMIC CELEBRATIONS AND FESTIVALS		
NAME OF FESTIVAL	**DATE IN ISLAM CALENDER**	**PURPOSE**
New Year, Day of *Hijra*	*Muharram*	To celebrate Muhammad's departure from Mecca to Medina.
Muhammad's birth	*Rabi I*	To celebrate Muhammad's birth.
Laila al-barh, the Night of Forgiveness	*Rajab*	Preparation for Ramadan. A month of fasting to draw closer to God.
Lailat al-qadr, the Night of Power	*Ramadan*	To commemorate Muhammad's receiving of the Qur'an.
Id al-fitr	*Shawwal*	The feast marking the end of Ramadan.
Dhu al-hijja	*Dhu al-Qadah*	The pilgrimage to Mecca.
Id ul-Adha, the Festival of Sacrifice	*Dhu al Hijja*	The closing festival of the pilgrimage to Mecca, celebrated worldwide.

Pilgrimages

The pilgrimage to Mecca

In order to fulfil the *hajj*, all Muslims hope to make a pilgrimage to Mecca (*Makkah*) where they engage in ceremonies which focus on the *Ka'aba*, a cube-shaped shrine which is supposed to have been built by Abraham and his son Ishmael.

The Black Stone

In one of the walls of the *Ka'aba* is the Black Stone, the most venerated Muslim object, which is said to have fallen out of heaven. One of the high points of the pilgrimage is to touch and kiss the Black Stone.

No non-Muslims may enter Mecca. All pilgrims wear similar clothes, traditionally made of two white sheets sown together (*ihram*), to show that in Allah's eyes they are all equal.

Arafat

Four ceremonies, known collectively as *Arafat*, are observed on the eighth, ninth and tenth days of the month in which the *hajj* takes place and are the climax of the whole pilgrimage.

1. Walking seven times round the *Ka'aba*, in an anti-clockwise direction.
2. Walking or running seven times between two nearby hills, al-Safa and al-Marwa.
3. Walking the 12-mile trip to Mount Arafat to assembly there on the ninth day. This is the site where

Muhammad preached his last sermon. On the way back to Mecca pilgrims throw stones at three pillars which represent Satan. On their return they make seven more circuits of the *Ka'aba*.

4. On the following day the Festival of Sacrifice (*Id ul-Adha*) is held on the following day at Mina, where sheep, goats or camels are sacrificed.

Malcolm X goes to Mecca

In 1964, after going to Mecca to perform *hajj*, El-Hajj Malik El-Shabazz, more popularly known as Malcolm X (the black-rights activist and religious leader) reverted to orthodox Islam. His new faith reflected his belief in brotherhood between blacks and whites.

Other well-known reverts to Islam include:

Muhammad Ali (formerly Cassius Clay)

This three-time heavyweight boxing champion of the world reverted to orthodox Islam in 1965. To this day, the boxer is the most widely recognized sports personality in the world.

Kareem Abdul-Jabbar (formerly Ferdinand Lewis Alcindor)

Alcindor reverted from Catholicism to Islam before the 1971-72 American baseball season. Before retiring in 1989, he spent 20 seasons playing for the Milwaukee Bucks and Los Angeles Lakers. He has six times been the most valuable player and is one of the 50 greatest players in NBA History.

Hamdan Chris Eubank

Hamdan Chris Eubank, British boxer. He reverted to Islam in March 1997, after defeating Camilo Alocon of Columbia at the Dubai Tennis Stadium in a light heavyweight contest. After his reversion

he took the name Hamdan.

Haiqa Khan
(formerly Jemimah Goldsmith)

Jewish daughter of billionaire Sir James Goldsmith. At the age of 21, she married the Pakistani cricketer Imran Khan, reverted to Islam and took a Muslim name.

F.A.Qs (Frequently Asked Questions) about Islam

Q: How many Muslims are there?
A: Islam is the fastest growing religion in America and in the world.

There are approximately 1.2 billion Muslims worldwide.

More than 20% of the world's population are Muslims.

Soon, one in four people will be Muslim.

If Muslims continue to increase as they have done in the past ten years, it is calculated that in the year 2010 Islam will overtake Christianity and become the major religion in the world.

Q: Where do Muslims live?
A: Muslims live in over 120 countries. They are the dominant population in 36 countries.

Q: Is there a color linked to Muslims?
A: Yes, green is the color of Islam and is used on their flags and banners.

B: Who are the Sufis?
A: Sufis, so-called because they wear coarse garments made from wool (suf), are Muslims noted for their dance, music and chanting, through which they reach out to Allah. Sufis are mystics and believe that it is possible to experience the truth of divine knowledge and love. The Whirling Dervishes of Turkey, renowned for their spectacular dances, are the best known Sufis.

Q: What is the difference between the Sunnis and the Shi'ites?

A: The Sunnis and the Shi'ites are the two main groups within Islam. Sunnis and Shi'ites agree about the basic teachings of Islam. Their disagreement centers on who was to be the leader (caliph) of the Muslims after Muhammad's death.

The Shi'ites thought that Muhammad's son-in-law, Ali, should be the first caliph. The Sunnis disagreed, claiming they were following the custom (*sunni*) example of the Prophet, and relying on "the consensus of the community" rather than a spiritual leader.

The Sunnis

About 90% of the world's Muslims are Sunnis.

The Shi'ites

Shi'a Muslims accept the authority of the *Imam*. As successor and descendant of Muhammad he can commit no sin and is an intermediary between man and God. Most of the Shi'ites live in Iran.

Q: To what extent do people like Osama bin Laden represent all Muslims?

A: He is not a traditional Muslim. He belongs to an extremist, puritan sect called the Wahhabis which was started in the eighteenth century by Muhammad ibn Abd at Wahhab. All music except drums was banned. Mosques were stripped of decoration. Wahhab was driven from Medina and traveled into the north-east Nejd where he converted the Saudis. The Saudi tribe waged war for over a century until the establishment of Saudi Arabia in 1932. Bin laden was exiled from Saudi Arabia because he vowed to destroy the Saudi royal family for allowing US troops on its soil after Desert Storm. The Taliban are a Wahhabi sect.

Q: Does Islam treat women harshly?

A: In various Islamic countries women are treated differently.

Saudi Arabia

In Saudi Arabia strict rules govern women's behavior.

- Women wear traditional dress, (the *burqa*) including a veil, so their whole bodies are covered.
- Women are not allowed to work.
- Women are not allowed to drive cars.

Syria

In Syria women are allowed to wear western clothes, work and study

"Men are in charge of women, because Allah hath made the one of them to excel the other, and because they spend of their property (for the support of women). So good women are the obedient, guarding in secret that which Allah hath guarded. As for those from whom ye fear rebellion, admonish them and banish them to beds apart, and scourge them." *Qur'an 4:34.59*

3 HINDUISM

CONTENTS	
	page

Introduction

After Christianity and Islam, Hinduism is the world's third largest religion. It is also the oldest of the four major world religions, and is often traced back to about 1500 BCE (although its earliest roots go back even further to about 7000 BCE), predating Islam by some 900 years. Buddhism, Jainism and Sikhism evolved from the Hindu religion. Hinduism remains the dominant religion in India where about 80% of the population are Hindus.

The sincere religious devotion inspired by Hindus is demonstrated each year as millions of Hindu pilgrims seek spiritual purification by bathing in the sacred waters of the River Ganges. The most auspicious moment to engage in this ritual bathing is at Allahabad during the great six-week long Kumbh Mela festival which takes place once every twelve years.

The logistics for the last festival, held in January 2001, were staggering. Erected especially for the occasion, along the river bank, was an 18-square-mile tent city with 15 pontoon bridges, 15,000 streetlights and what is thought to have been the world's most extensive loudspeaker system. 20,000 police were on hand to keep order and locate the 30,000 people who, according to CNN, were separated from their families in the chaos.

It was expected that over 45 million people, ranging from national leaders to poor villagers, would converge at the holy confluence of the rivers (*Sangam*), Ganga, Yamuna and Saraswati (the invisible river). In the event, an estimated 75 million took part in the festival, the largest number of people ever to gather in one place.

A family of religions

Hinduism is the name given to a family of religions and cultures that began and still flourish in India.

Together, the diverse beliefs of Jainism, Sanatana, Buddhism and later additions (like Sikhism) constitute the Hindu religions of India. Sanatana Dharma – one of the Hindu religions – is wrongly understood by westerners to be synonymous with the Hindu religion. This chapter follows the western use of the word "Hindu" and wherever the word appears in the context of religion, it should be understood as Sanatana Dharma.

Over 700 million Hindus in the world today follow the Sanatana Dharma.

Origins of Hinduism

Oldest religion

Hinduism, the third largest world religion, claims to be the oldest religion in the world, dating back to prehistoric times. It embraces the religious beliefs and institutions of most of the inhabitants of India. But Hinduism does not have a formal creed; it is a way of life that has developed over the past 5,000 years.

When was Hinduism founded?

Hinduism does not owe its existence to any single historic event. Rather, it is a complex religion that has continually evolved over thousands of years. Because the early inhabitants of the Indus Valley practiced a religion which had several features in common with modern Hinduism, the beginnings of Hinduism have been dated back to the time when that civilization flourished – approximately 2500 BCE.

Its origin: a people

Hindus do not use the word "Hinduism" and the first known use of the word "Hinduism" goes back to only 1829. Technically, "Hindu" is not the name of a religion but a people. It is a Persian word which means "Indian." The term Hindu comes from the name of the river Indus, which flows 1,800 miles from Tibet through Kashmir and Pakistan to the sea.

In antiquity, when the Persians conquered northwest India, they did not know what to call the people of the region and so gave them the name

Hindu, a mispronunciation of the word Sindhu (the river Indus). Thus the people living around and on the east of Sindhu (the Indians) became Hindus and the best translation of Hindu would be Indian (people of the subcontinent of India).

The religion of India

The religion of India has its roots in a blend of spiritual beliefs: those of the ancient Indians from the Indus civilization (Dravirs) and those of newcomers, the Aryans (nomadic tribes who lived in central Asia and came to India between about 1800 BCE and 1500 BCE, coinciding with the end of the Indus civilization).

Name of the religion

This early fusion of religious beliefs is correctly called *Sanatana Dharma*, "eternal religion," because it dealt with the relation between *Atman* (soul) and God (supreme soul). It is sometimes also called *Vaidika Dharma*, religion of the "Vedas;" the Vedas being its first religious writings.

Hinduism and other religions

Hinduism differs from Christianity and other Western religions.

- Its concept of God does not have a central place.
- It does not have a single source of authority.
- It does not have a founder.
- It is not prophetic.
- It does not have a specific theological system.
- It does not have a single system of morality.
- It does not have a central religious organization.
- It does not have one scripture which alone is authoritative.

Hinduism at a glance

Hinduism consists of thousands of different religious groups that have evolved in India since 1500 BCE. It is so diverse that it is not easy to define, but Hinduism can be said to include the following elements:

- ### Worship of gods
  Hindus believe in one supreme God

(Brahma) expressed in various forms or aspects. It is these aspects that are worshiped as gods.

- ### The Vedas
  While Hindus may rarely read their earliest scriptures, they still revere them.

- ### A way of life
  Hindus do not separate religion from other aspects of life. For Hindus in India, Hinduism is an inextricable part of their existence, a complete approach to life that involves social class, earning a living, family, politics, diet, as well as prayer, worship and the holding of religious festivals and feasts.

- ### Toleration
  Hinduism has a deserved reputation for being highly tolerant of other religions. Hindus have a saying:

  > "*Ekam Sataha Vipraha Bahudha Vadanti.*"
  > "The truth is One, but different sages call it by different names."

Hindus respect Jesus as a spiritual person and do not demonize him as Christians and Muslims demonize the Hindu gods and goddesses. This tolerance has created a faith in India that is inclusive, unlike the exclusive religions of the west. The Hindu accepts all religions as paths to the same goal.

Hindu scriptures

Hindu scriptures

- The Vedas
- The Upanishads
- Mahabharata, containing The Bhagavad Gita
- Ramayana

The Vedas

The most ancient sacred texts of the Hindu religion are written in Sanskrit and called the Vedas (vedah means "knowledge"). The Vedas are said to have existed for ever, and the date they are given, approximately 1500 BCE, is merely the date they were written down.

The Vedas contain accounts of creation, information on ritual sacrifices and prayers to the deities. Hindus accept that the Vedas contain the truths of their religion and while many may not read these texts, they nevertheless venerate them. The four Vedic books are:

- Rig Veda
- Sama Veda
- Yajur Veda
- Atharva Veda.

The Rig Veda

The Rig Veda ("Wisdom of the Verses") is not only the oldest work of literature in any Indo-European language, it is the oldest religious literature in the world.

The Rig Veda has 1,028 hymns addressed to gods. These Vedic gods were personifications of natural forces.

The Sama Veda

These verses were designed to be chanted.

The Yajur Veda

The book contains instructions, in prose, for carrying out rituals.

The Atharva Veda

Rites and spells for curing illness are given in verse.

Upanishads

The Upanishads were originally written in Sanskrit (800–400 BCE). Written as commentaries on the Vedic texts, they speculate on the origin of the universe, the nature of deity, and *atman* (the individual soul) and its relationship to Brahman (the universal soul). They introduce the doctrine of karma and recommend meditation and the practice of yoga. These teachings are told by gurus (teachers) to their pupils in the form of parables and stories.

Praying

Hindus use their scriptures in their meditations and prayers.

Actions

"As one acts and conducts himself, so does he become. The doer of good becomes good. The doer of evil becomes evil. One becomes virtuous by virtuous action, bad by bad action." *Veda Upanishads*

Duty

"Let there be no neglect of the duties to the Gods and the fathers.
Be one to whom the mother is a God.
Be one to whom the father is a God.
Be one to whom the teacher is a God.
Be one to whom the guest is a God."
Krishna Yajur Veda, Taittiriya Upanishad 1.11.1-2

Desire

"You are what your deep driving desire is." *Brihadaranyaka Upanishad*

Dreamless sleep

"As an eagle, weary after soaring in the sky, folds its wings and flies down to rest in its nest, so does the shining Self enter the state of dreamless sleep, where one is freed from all desires." *Brihadaranyaka Upanishad*

Freedom

"If men thought of God as much as they think of the world, who would not attain liberation?
Maitri Upanishad 6.24

Reality

"From Unreality, lead me to Reality,
From Darkness, lead me unto Light,
From Death, lead me to Immortality."
Brihad-Aranyaka Upanishad

The self

"As the spider moves along the thread, as small sparks come forth from the fire, even so from this Self come forth all breaths, all worlds, all divinities, all beings.
Brihadaranyaka, Upanishad 2,1,20

Truth

"He who has found Truth, seeks no more; the riddle is solved; desire is gone, he is at peace.
Having approached from everywhere that which is everywhere, whole, he passes into the Whole." *Mundaka Upanishad*

The epics

Hindu epics contain legendary stories about gods and humans.

The two major epics are very long poems: the Mahabharata, which has 24,000 verses, and the Ramayana which has 100,000 verses.

The Puranas detail myths of Hindu gods and heroes and also comment on religious practice and cosmology. They contain 18 poems, six for Vishnu, six for Shiva and six for Brahma.

The Bhagavad Gita

The Bhagavad Gita, the "Song of the Lord," is part of the great epic, the Mahabharata.

Its 18 chapters and 700 verses are the most popular and most important of the Hindu scriptures.

The story

The Bhagavad Gita is a poem describing a conversation between a noble warrior, Arjuna, and his charioteer, Krishna. It takes place when Arjuna, suddenly overcome by sorrow in the middle of a battle field, stands confused and withdrawn. Moved by extreme compassion and love, Lord Krishna teaches Arjuna the paths of

- right action,
- right knowledge and
- right devotion.

Its principles

This book sets out, in story form, the correct way to behave and think. One should:

- be devoted to the form of God known as Krishna
- trust Krishna totally.

"Make every act an offering to me (God); regard me as your only protector. Relying on interior discipline, meditate on me always. Remembering me, you shall overcome all difficulties through my grace. But if you will not heed me in your self-will, nothing will avail you."
The Bhagavad Gita

The moral

The Bhagavad Gita teaches one how to live in this world and yet remain like lotus leaves floating on water. The world in which a Hindu lives is said to be a world of illusion. Out of ignorance and egoism the self is bound to this world through desires and actions, not knowing its true nature and true purpose. According to this teaching the Hindu needs to be released from the cycle of births and deaths and the forces of nature to which he is chained.

Duty

A person should not be inactive or neglect his duty. He should do his duty:

- with a sense of detachment;
- with a steady mind and with self-discipline, casting away egoism and all other negative qualities;
- without any desire to gain a reward;
- with a sense of sacrifice, completely surrendering to God and fully devoted to him.

Detachment

The Bhagavad Gita teaches how to escape from the human predicament, not by avoiding the responsibilities of the worldly life, but by facing them with a sense of fearlessness and detachment.

"The man who, having abandoned all desires, goes onward without attachments, free from selfishness and vanity, attains to peace. This is the Brahma state, O son of Pritha! he who has attained it is troubled no more." *The Bhagavad Gita*

"By acting without attachment a man reaches what is far away." *The Bhagavad Gita*

"Do your work the same in success and misfortune. This evenness – that is discipline." *The Bhagavad Gita*

Salvation

According to The Bhagavad Gita, salvation is not possible for those who want to escape from life and activity. The way of salvation is to live a life of sacrifice which is fully surrendered to God.

Union with the Supreme

Those who are prepared to go through the battles of life with self-discipline and who have surrendered themselves to God with complete devotion are qualified to attain liberation and union with the Supreme.

The Source

I am the One Source of all:
the evolution of all comes from Me.
I am beginningless, unborn,
the Lord of the worlds.
I am the soul which dwells in the heart of all things.
I am the beginning, the middle and the end of all that lives.
I am the seed of all things that are:
and no being that moves or
moves not can ever be without me.
In any way that men love Me
In that same way they find My love;
For many are the paths of men,
But they all in the end come to Me.
Krishna, from The Bhagavad Gita

Hindu beliefs

One God and many gods

Hindus acknowledge and worship various gods, but these are all aspects of the one supreme God. The gods Vishnu, Shiva and Brahma are different forms and names of the one God. Vishnu, in particular, has appeared on earth in various forms. Among these Krishna and Rama are especially loved and worshiped.

Polytheistic?

Many non-Hindus accuse Hinduism of being polytheistic (of worshiping many gods). Hindus reply that they actually believe in only one supreme God, called "Brahman".

Brahman

According to Hindu beliefs, Brahman is the principle and source of the universe. In Hinduism the principle of Brahman, the ultimate reality or One that is All, is a central belief. This divine intelligence pervades all beings including the individual soul. Hindus believe that the entire universe is one divine entity who is at one with the universe while simultaneously transcending it.

The many Hindu deities are manifestations of the one Brahman.

Brahman is a supreme spirit that permeates everything.

But Brahman is not a being in the sense that Christians think of God as a being.

Brahman is entirely impersonal, and entirely impossible to describe.

Everything, including each human being, in the universe is part of Brahman, but Brahman is more than the sum of everything in the universe.

There is only one ultimate reality – Brahman.

But that ultimate reality shows itself in many forms, and some of those forms are called gods.

Trimurti

In Hinduism there is the concept of one God with three aspects or forms, the *Trimurti*, or Hindu Trinity. Each aspect is given physical representation.

- Brahma reflects God's divine work of creating the universe;
- Vishnu reflects God's work in keeping the universe in existence;
- Shiva reflects God's work in destroying it.

Four denominations

Hinduism has four primary denominations:

- Shivaism
- Vaishnavism
- Shaktism
- Smaritism.

The majority of Hindus either follow Vaishnavaism, which regards Vishnu as the ultimate deity, or Shivaism, which regards Shiva as the ultimate deity.

Generally held beliefs

There are no set rules for being a Hindu. Hinduism does not have a single creed which it regularly recites. Because Hinduism includes a very wide range of beliefs and practices, there are few things that are common to all Hindu groups. The most commonly held beliefs are:

- a belief in a single divinity or supreme God that is present in everything;
- a belief in other gods who are aspects of that supreme God;
- a belief that the soul repeatedly goes through a cycle of being: birth into a body, death and rebirth;
- a belief in *karma*, a force that determines the quality of each life, depending on how well one behaved in a past life;
- a belief that *dharma* must be fulfilled;
- vegetarianism; many Hindus are vegetarians, believing in reverence for life and non-violence to all living things.

However, a Hindu may question the holy scriptures and even question the gods.

Who is a Hindu?

Hinduism is more than a highly organized religious and social system, it is a way of life. "Acceptance of the Vedas with reverence; recognition of the fact that the means or ways to salvation are diverse; and the realization of the truth that the number of gods to be worshiped is large, that indeed is the distinguishing feature of the Hindu religion."
B. G. Tilak's definition of what makes one a basic Hindu, as quoted by India's Supreme Court, July 2, 1995

Four goals

Hindus organize their lives around certain activities or purusharthas. These have been called "the four aims of Hinduism" or "the doctrine of the fourfold end of life." There are four legitimate goals in life (*purusharthas*):

- *dharma* (appropriate living)
- *artha* (the pursuit of material gain by lawful means)
- *kama* (delight of the senses)
- *moksha* (release from rebirth).

Four duties

Each Hindu has four daily duties. He must:

- revere the deities
- respect ancestors
- respect all beings
- honor all humankind.

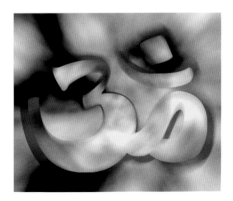

Reincarnation

Dharma

Dharma means:

- religion
- law
- duty
- eternal order
- righteousness.

Living or acting in the right way is known as *dharma* so the Indian name for the religion of India is Sanatana Dharma (meaning "everlasting dharma").

If you keep the rules of *dharma* you avoid wrongdoing and acquire merit.

Samsara

Hindus believe that the universe has no beginning or ending, but is cyclical. *Samsara* (literally, "stream of existence") is the Sanskrit word for the cycle of life which consists of birth, death and then rebirth. All Hindus believe that the individual soul exists in this cycle of birth into a body, followed by death and then rebirth.

Samsara refers to the transmigration of the soul and its constant rebirth by the law of *karma*.

Moksha

The ultimate aim of all Hindus is to escape from this cycle of birth and death and rebirth. This liberation is called *moksha*, a kind of salvation.

If a person takes good actions in life and thus builds good *karma*, he or she will be born into a better life in the next incarnation. This cycle of birth and death continues until the person attains *moksha*.

Karma

Hinduism is the only religion which teaches the law of *karma*. This is the belief that the quality of the next life depends on the soul's *karma* – that is, the goodness or badness of deeds done in this life.

Karma is the accumulated sum of one's good and bad deeds.

Through pure acts, thoughts and devotion one can be reborn at a higher level.

Bad deeds can cause a person to be reborn at a lower level or even as an animal.

The unequal distribution of wealth, prestige and suffering are thus seen as natural consequences of one's previous acts, both in this life and in previous lives.

The law of *karma*

For every action one takes, good or bad, there will be a good or bad reaction in the future, which could be in a few seconds, in 20 years or in one's next incarnation. This is the law of *karma*.

Good actions

If you take good actions, you will face good reactions. This may come in the form of good health, wealth or birth on a higher plane.

A life devoted to Yoga assit Hindus in this quest.

Bad actions

If you take bad actions, you will face bad reactions in the future. The bad reactions may come in the form of disease, poverty or birth on a lower plane.

Bad *karma*

Actions which result in bad *karma*:

- eating meat
- violence
- ignorance
- harshness
- untruthfulness
- lust
- anger
- greed
- attachments
- desires
- gambling
- pleasing oneself at the expense of others
- alcohol.

Good *karma*

Actions which build good *karma*:

- vegetarianism
- non-violence
- generosity
- charity
- self-control
- truthfulness
- simplicity
- forgiveness
- cleanliness
- being free from attachments, desires and selfishness.

Your destiny is in your own hands

The law of *karma* teaches that you are held responsible for all your actions. The reason why some people suffer more than others is that they sinned more than others in their past and thus they are now facing the bad reactions to the bad actions taken in their past.

The reason why some good people suffer all their life is because, although they are now good, they still suffer because they are facing the bad reactions to the bad actions taken in their previous lives. But because they are now taking good actions they will face good reactions (be happy) in their next life.

Transmigration of the soul

When someone dies, that person's soul is reborn into a new body (not necessarily a human body). The whole process of the soul being reborn into a new body is called reincarnation, sometimes referred to as the repetitious transmigration of the soul. Hinduism is based on this concept of reincarnation in which all living beings, from plants on earth to gods above, are caught in a cosmic cycle of becoming and perishing until *moksha* is achieved.

The argument for belief in reincarnation

The argument centers on the conviction that God is just. The opposite of belief in reincarnation is the view that every person has only one life.

In life there are manifest inequalities: some people are born rich and healthy, while others are born in suffering and poverty.

If each person has only one life, then life is unfair.

But God is just; it is against his nature to be unfair. He cannot allow innocent people to suffer.

It is only just that a person's present state should be the result of that person's actions, and therefore when people are born unequal it must be because of actions in a previous life.

The soul passes into another body at death

"Never was there a time when I did not exist, nor you, nor all these kings; nor in the future shall any of us cease to be. As the embodied soul continuously passes, in the body from childhood to youth to old age, the soul similarly passes into another body at death. A sober person is not bewildered by such a change." *Lord Krishna (Bg. 2.12-13)*

"As a person puts on new garments, giving up old ones, the soul similarly accepts new material bodies, giving up the old and useless ones." *Lord Krishna (Bg. 2.22)*

"When one dies in the mode of goodness, he attains to the pure higher planets of the great sages. When one dies in the mode of passion, he takes birth among those engaged in fruitive activities; and when one dies in the mode of ignorance, he takes birth in the animal kingdom." *Lord Krishna*

Three paths to salvation

Although there is agreement that obtaining *moksha* is the ultimate goal of any practicing Hindu, there is much disagreement on the ways or paths (magna) which should be taken to obtain release from the cycles of life and death.

Three paths to salvation are set out in The Bhagavad Gita:

- Duty
- Devotion
- Knowledge.

1. The first path, *karma marga*

"The Path of Duties," is the way of action. This teaches that one should carry out one's duties in society.

2. The second path, *bhakti-marga* "The Path of Devotion," involves becoming devoted and faithful to a personal god. In this devotional approach to salvation, God is no longer an impersonal Brahman, but is approachable and may be reverently worshiped. Krishna said, "Only by *bhakti* can men see me and know me and come to me."

3. The third path, *jnana-marga* "The Path of Knowledge," achieves union with God through the assistance of yoga, meditation, and repeating the mantra "Om."

The Hindu deities

Hindu gods

Hindus believe in a supreme soul or spirit called Brahman which has no form or shape. In the Veda, Brahman is beyond definition but is said to be the ultimate One.

Brahman's power and other characteristics are represented by the many Hindu gods and goddesses. According to the epic Mahabharata (1.1.39), there are 33,333 Hindu deities.

Hindus may worship just one God, or many, or none of the gods.

The Vedic deities

The deities described in the Vedas are not only forces of nature but also forces within the human body that help each person to overcome impediments and make spiritual progress. Spiritual perfection cannot be attained without the development of these inner godheads.

Hindu Deities
The great Gods

These deities form the core of Hindu belief.

- Brahma, the Creator. Very few temples are dedicated to him as he is beyond worship.
- Vishnu, the Preserver and Protector. Through his ten incarnations (*avatars*) he comes close to humans.
- Lakshmi, Vishnu's wife, the goddess of love and beauty.
- Shiva, the Powerful God, the Destroyer.

- Sarasvati, consort of Brahma. The goddess of knowledge and learning.

The gods of the Vedas

- Indra, the sky-god, administrator in chief of heaven.
- Surya, the Sun god.
- Agni, the god of fire and sacrifice who is the life-force of nature.
- Vayu, the god of wind.
- Varuna, the god of rains. He has power to reward or punish and upholds the cosmic order.
- Yama, the god of death.
- Kubera, the god of material wealth.
- Soma, the god of the moon.

Sons and relatives

In order to preserve the ancient culture and tradition, many great leaders of the past, such as Shivaji and Tilak, popularized deities. The inherently plural nature of Hinduism easily accommodated the new forms of gods and Indians took to their worship in great numbers.

Some of these new gods were:

- Ganesh, son of Shiva and Parvati.
- Kartikeya, son of Shiva and Parvati.
- Krishna, son of Vasudeva, brother of Balarama. Krishna is the most popular of the gods as well as hero of many myths, where he is a king, lover or warrior.
- Hanuman, son of Vayu.

Vishnu's incarnations

In medieval India, many saints fought against the evils of the caste system and gave rise to the immensely popular cults of Vaishnavism or worship of Vishnu. The following are the various forms or *avatars* which Lord Vishnu is said to have taken to rescue his followers:

- Matsya, Vishnu as a fish. He saved Manu (the first man) from the great flood.
- Kurma, Vishnu as a tortoise. He recovered ambrosia (food for the gods) that had been lost in the flood.
- Varaha, Vishnu as a boar. He rescued the earth from the cosmic ocean where the demons had thrown her.
- Narasimha, the lion-man. He killed the demon Hiranyakashipu.
- Vamana, the dwarf. He defeated evil demons.
- Parashu Rama, Rama with an axe. He defeated the warrior *kshatriyas* 21 times.
- Rama Chandra. He killed Rvana, the demon of Sri Lanka.
- Krishna. He is also a god in his own right.

- Buddha, the completely enlightened one. The ninth *avatar* is the founder of Buddhism, Gautama the Buddha.
- Kalki. Kalki has already had nine avatars, and his tenth avatar is yet to come.

From these ten *avatars* of Vishnu, only Rama, Krishna and Buddha are followed today.

Idols

Hindu deities are represented in idols. The idols in themselves are not worshiped but worship is offered to the god they represent. Most Hindus worship at home and have a shrine there. Hindu temples are the focus of religious life, but there is not a strong tradition of corporate congregational worship.

Praying to the gods

When Hindus pray they usually pray before a picture or statue of a god on which they focus their thoughts.

Each Hindu temple (*mandir*) is dedicated to a particular god or goddess. This is the deity's earthly home, an earthly replica of his heavenly home. In the innermost and holiest part of the temple, a shrine houses the god or goddess.

Shrines, often consisting just of a statue or picture of the deity, are not only to be found in temples, but are seen everywhere in India. There are shrines on countless street corners.

Worship

Meditation is often practiced, with yoga being the most common system. Other activities include:

- daily prayers,
- public rituals, and
- *puja*, a ceremonial dinner for a god.

Celebrations of life

The practice of Hinduism includes rites and ceremonies centering on birth, marriage and death. Ceremonies known as Samskaras mark the milestones in a Hindu's life.

Birth

When a baby is ten days old he is taken to a naming ceremony at which his horoscope is drawn up by a priest.

Adulthood

At the age of nine or ten Hindus from the top three castes attend a ceremony at which they are given a long loop of cotton (a sacred thread) to wear. This marks the beginning of their adult life.

Marriage

Hindu weddings involve long ceremonies and feasting.

Death

At death a Hindu is not buried but is cremated. In this way his soul is taken to heaven by the sacred fire and here he is reborn.

Festivals

Hinduism claims to have more festivals than any other religion. In India 15 festivals are celebrated annually in at least six states and a festival of some sort is celebrated every day. Hindus however do not celebrate all the festivals. Most celebrate three major festivals each year, when they visit a temple, have special meals and exchange gifts. The birthday of a god or goddess, a family event or the harvest are popular festivals.

Holi

This is the most colorful and happy of the Hindu festivals. It is dedicated to Krishna who disguised himself as a cowherd in order to have fun with the milkmaids. The festival is a time for dancing and bonfires and everyone, regardless of age, caste or belief, can join in.

Dussehra

Dusshera ("the tenth") comes the day after Navaratri (nine nights) and is a ten-day celebration held in honor of Kali. This festival, marked by dancing and processions, celebrates Rama's triumph over the evil Ravana.

Divali

Divali ("Row of lights") is the festival of Lights marking the end of one year and the dawn of the new year. It is the most important festival in India and lasts for two to five days. Held in honor of the goddess of good fortune, Lakshmi, homes are decorated with rows of lamps symbolizing light and the victory of goodness.

Visiting a temple

Outside most temples a stall sells different types of *prasad* (gifts) which worshipers offer to the deity inside.

As a sign of respect before entering a temple, women cover their heads and everyone takes off their shoes.

As well as praying, Hindus have a *darshana* (viewing) of the statue which represents the deity.

Puja

Puja, the Indian word for worship, is a ceremonial dinner for a god.

Before *puja*

Bathing of the body symbolizes outer purification. Mantras and stotras are said for inner purification.

During *puja*

Hindus take their gifts (*prasad*) of fruit, flowers or incense and the priests present these to the god or goddess to be blessed. Then the priests give the gifts back to the worshipers and mark their foreheads with a *tilaka*, a red mark of blessing.

The scent of flowers signifies the flavor of the soul. The flowers are picked up with the right hand with the fingers pointed downwards and the flowers are dropped at the feet of the god. The fingers represent the five senses and their downward direction shows that the senses that are usually directed outwards are now directed inwards and downwards in submission.

When the flowers are dropped, the word *namah* is uttered. *Namah* is generally spoken as a greeting, but it is actually a corruption of "*na mama*" which means "not mine." Here the *pujari* (worshiper) is offering his soul, senses and everything but is acknowledging that it is not really his. Everything belongs to the god.

Pilgrimages

Pilgrimages (*tirthayatra*) to holy rivers (*tirtha*) and other places are among the most remarkable aspects of Indian religious life. By making a pilgrimage Hindus acquire merit and a good karma.

Hinduism has tens of thousands of holy places, all within the sub-continent of India. The major places of pilgrimage are linked to the gods Shiva, Krishna and Vishnu – and to the River Ganges – the most sacred river in India which is said to purify all who bathe in it.

Every 12 years in January or February millions of Hindu pilgrims gather on the banks of the River Ganges at Allahabad to celebrate the great bathing festival – Kumbh Mela. At the last gathering, in 2001, the pilgrims formed the world's largest congregation of worshipers.

The caste system and Gandhi

The caste system

Caste is the Indian class system. The caste system is not part of the original Hindu religion and is officially rejected by Hinduism. Although the caste system was abolished by law in 1949, it remains a significant force throughout India. A soul can be born into a different caste in the process of reincarnation. Marriages between castes are rare.

Four groups

Orthodox Hindu society in India was divided into four major hereditary classes:

- Brahmins (priests and educated class)
- Kshatriya (professional, governing and military class)
- Vaisahya (landowners, farmers and merchants)
- Sudra (peasants and laborers).

Brahma

According to Hindu tradition each caste came, symbolically, from a different part of Brahma's body:

- the Brahmins from his mouth,
- the Kshatriyas from his arms,
- the Vaishyas from his thighs, and
- the Sudras from his feet.

Untouchables

Below the Sudra was a fifth group, the Untouchables (so-called because those who belonged to the other four castes thought that they would be polluted if they touched them) who were condemned to carry out the lowest menial occupations and had no social standing.

Gandhi

Influential Hindus

Rammohan Roy (1772–1833) is known as "the father of modern India" because of his attempts to reform Hinduism.

Sri Ramakriashna (1836–86) reformed and revived Hinduism. After his death one of his followers founded the Ramakrishna mission which is active both in India and in other countries and is known for its contribution to scholarship and humanitarian works.

Rabindranath Tagore (1861–1941) awarded the Nobel Prize for Literature in 1913 is still influential through his poetry.

Gandhi gave his followers this rule for life:

"I shall not fear anyone on earth; I shall fear only God. I shall not bear ill-will toward anyone. I shall not submit to injustice from anyone. I shall conquer untruth by truth and in resisting untruth I shall put up with all suffering."

And about Untouchables he said:

"If I have to be reborn, I would wish to be born an Untouchable, so that I might share their sorrows, their sufferings and the affronts levelled at them, in order that I might endeavor to free myself and them from this miserable condition." *Gandhi*

FACTFILE ON GANDHI	
Gandhi's Hinduism was all-embracing. He once said of himself, "I am a Muslim, a Sikh, a Christian and a Jew."	
1869	Mohandas Karamchand Gandhi born in Porbandar in Gujarat.
1893	Gandhi goes to Johannesburg to practice law but is thrown out because he is colored.
1906	Launches a campaign of nonviolent resistance (satyagraha).
1913	In Transvaal, South Africa, leads 2,500 Indians in a campaign of passive resistance against the whites for their mistreatment of Asian immigrants.
1914	Returns to India and conducts the first of 14 fasts as a method of political protest.
1930	A civil disobedience campaign against the British in India begins on March 12. The All-India Trade Congress asks Gandhi, who is now called Mahatma (meaning "great soul" and used as a mark of respect), to lead the demonstrations. Gandhi heads up a 165-mile march to the Gujarat Coast of the Arabian Sea and produces salt by evaporation of sea water in violation of the law, as a gesture of defiance against the British monopoly in salt production.
1932	Gandhi begins a "fast unto death" to protest against the British government's mistreatment of India's lowest caste, the Untouchables, whom Gandhi calls Harijans, "God's children." After 6 days of fasting he obtains a pact that improves the status of the Untouchables.
1947	India becomes free from 200 years of British rule. A major victory for Gandhian principles of non-violence.
1948	On January 30, Gandhi is assassinated by Nathuram Godse, a Hindu fanatic, at a prayer meeting.

F.A.Qs (Frequently Asked Questions) about Hinduism

Q: Where do Hindus live?
A: Mainly in India where about 80% of Indians are Hindus.

Nepal where 89% follow Hinduism.

Over 10% of the population in Bangladesh are Hindu.

Indonesia, Sri Lanka, Pakistan and Malaysia also have large Hindu populations.

There are just over one million Hindus in the United States.

Q: How many Hindus are there?
A: In 2000 there were nearly 800 million Hindus worldwide.

13% of the world's population is Hindu.

Q: What for a Hindu is religion?
A: Religion is:

- a way of life
- a heritage
- a tradition
- a right way of thinking
- a way to live in this life which ensures a better in the next reincarnation.

Q: Who are sadhus?
A: Sadhus are the holy men of India. They give up their homes and possessions in order to live a life of meditation and prayer. Other Hindus provide them with food and money.

Followers of Vishnu have three vertical lines of ash smeared on their foreheads.

Followers of Shiva have three horizontal lines of ash smeared on their foreheads.

Q: Who are gurus?
A: Gurus ("teachers") are spiritual teachers and guides in the religions of India. They teach mantras and techniques of meditation.

Q: Why do cows roam freely in the streets in India?
A: The cow is a sacred animal. Although all animals and living beings are sacred to the Hindu because God is present in all creatures, the cow has a special place in the hearts of Hindus. The cow is thought to be a living symbol of Mother Earth who bestows blessing on the earth and it is therefore an act of worship just to feed a cow.

Q: What does a red dot mean on a forehead?
A: This dot, called a *vindia* or a *teep*, signifies that the wearer is a Hindu. A black dot indicates that the girl is unmarried and a red dot that she is married. This practice probably goes back to the Indus civilization in the third millennium BCE.

Q: What is "Om"?
A: Hindus acquire special knowledge by meditation through yoga and by repeating the mantra "Om." Prolonged repetition of this mantra induces a trance-like state in which the worshiper may be united to Brahma.

The *mala*, akin to a rosary, is a string of 108 beads which is fingered while the word "Om" and the name of God are uttered. Such repetition is known as *japa*.

Q: What is yoga?

A: Hindus use yoga as a way to become united with Brahma. The eight traditional stages in yoga are:

- restraint
- discipline
- posture
- breathing
- detachment
- concentration
- meditation
- trance.

Q: What is the Evil Eye?

A: All misfortune is attributed to the Evil Eye which, it is believed, can cause injury when called upon by the exercise of magic. It is thought to be an ever-present threat and is constantly to be countered.

4 BUDDHISM

CONTENTS	
	page

Introduction

Defining Buddhism

Buddhism is a diverse body of
- religion,
- philosophy, and
- cultural practice.

It is native to India, and characterized by a belief in reincarnation and a supreme being of many forms and natures.

Buddhism is the fourth largest world religion. While it is not easy to estimate the exact number of Buddhists, since "Buddhism" is often used as a blanket term to include a wide variety of religious beliefs that are not, strictly speaking, Buddhist, the number is probably about 400,000,000. In the USA there are over half a million Buddhists.

For the last two centuries Buddhism has shown an ability to communicate across diverse cultural and national barriers. Despite the onslaughts of revolutions, commercialism, and western technology Buddhist teaching and its ancient meditation techniques have continued to attract millions of adherents. As a result, unlike Christianity, Buddhism is growing at about the same rate as the world's population.

Prince Guatama Siddhartha, the Buddha (the word means "the enlightened one"), founded Buddhism in the fifth century BC. His followers today still base their beliefs on the summary of his teaching found in his Four Noble Truths.

Many non-Buddhists find themselves attracted to Buddhist beliefs seeing in the idea of *nirvana* (which means "the blowing out" of the fires of all desires as the self is absorbed into the infinite) a preferable alternative to the rat race into which most people are locked. It has been suggested that the moment may well be ripe for Buddhism to gently conquer more and more people who find themselves dissatisfied with materialism.

The founder of Buddhism

The roots of the religious and philosophical tradition of Buddhism stretch back over 2,500 years.

Siddhartha Gautama

In about 563 BCE Siddhartha Gautama, the founder of Buddhism, was born in Nepal.

Names given to Buddha

Siddhartha

Siddhartha means "One whose aim is accomplished," or, "He who has reached his goal." This is the name given to him by his father, King Suddhodana, and mother, Queen Mahamaya.

Gautama

Gautama was a second name. Members of noble Indian families usually chose a second name for themselves.

Kinsman

Kinsman of the Sun. His family traced their descent from the sun.

FACT FILE ON SIDDHARTHA GAUTAMA	
c. 563 BCE	Born in Nepal.
c. 537 BCE	Aged 16, marries Yasodharo.
534 BCE	Has a spiritual crisis after seeing suffering and death and leaves his palace for the life of a homeless, holy man.
528 BCE	Takes the name Buddha.
483 BCE	Buddha dies.

Sage

Sage of the Sakyans, Sakyamuni. His family were also members of the Sakya clan.

Buddha

Buddha means "the Awakened one" or "Enlightened one," or "One who has woken up." Gautama took the name of Buddha in 531 BCE.

Three palaces

Gautama, the son of a wealthy *rajan* (chieftan), was born in Lumbini, a village in Kapikvastri on the Indian-Nepalese border.

His father, a Hindu, did not have just one palace, but three, one for the cold season, one for the hot season, and one for the rainy season.

When Gautama was born it was prophesied that he would become a holy man, but his father did everything in his power to make sure this would never happen.

He surrounded his son with everything that was beautiful and pleasurable and made sure that his every whim was attended to.

But nothing fully satisfied Gautama. He found no deep happiness in his life. He married a beautiful wife, but he called their son Rahula ("the fetter" or, "the chain") because he felt that he was chained to a life of unsatisfying luxury.

Life-changing sights

Gautama's father gave orders that whenever his son wanted to go out for a ride in the coach, the roadway should be cleared of any sight that might upset him. But without his father's knowledge, Gautama went for four drives that changed his life.

He saw three frightening sights:

- On his first journey he saw a frail old man.
- On his second journey he saw a seriously ill man.
- On his third journe, he saw a dead man, and a funeral procession. His coachman assured him that suffering and death happened to everyone. Gautama was amazed to discover that life was full of suffering.
- On his fourth journey he saw a man in a yellow robe with a shaven head who looked content with life even though all he had was a begging bowl.

As a Hindu, Gautama had been taught to believe in reincarnation and the unending sequence of lives on this earth. Unable to bear that thought he sought the counsel of a holy man who told him that if he joined other holy men he would escape from earthly life forever.

Gautama renounces materialism

After viewing suffering and death Gautama, without saying goodbye to his wife and child, left his palace in the middle of the night with one servant. At dawn by a river he cut off his hair, gave his servant his sword, his jewels and his horse and went on alone on foot. When he met a beggar he exchanged his fine clothes for the beggar's rags.

Then Gautama looked for a teaching that would show him how he could break the cycle of reincarnation.

He was taught by the sage Alara Kalama.

He lived with some Brahmans but found their teaching most unappealing.

He engaged in severe yoga exercises but nearly starved to death.

He then meditated alone under a pipal tree.

A new religion

Seeing the light

After sitting in meditation for 49 day in
Bodh Gaya on the banks of the
Nairangana in Northern Indias under a
pipal tree (or fig-tree which later became
known as "the tree of enlightenment" or
bodhi-tree), Gautama had three visions.

First night

He had a vision which showed him his
past lives.

Second night

He had a vision in which he had
enlightenment about the cycle of birth,
death and rebirth.

On this night Gautama meditated on
the ten Great Virtues (*paramitas*) he had
achieved in his past lives:

- charity
- morality
- renunciation
- wisdom
- effort
- patience
- truth
- determination
- universal love
- equanimity.

Buddhist tradition states that the evil
tempter, Mara, did all he could to
prevent Gautama's enlightenment,
seeking to focus his attention on his ten
"armies:"

- lust
- hatred of the higher existence
- hunger and thirst
- craving
- laziness
- cowardice
- doubt
- hypocrisy
- seeking the praise of men
- exalting the self while despising
  others.

Gautama defeated Mara who then left
him to his visions.

Third night
The four noble truths were revealed to Gautama.

Enlightenment
In this way Gautama gained enlightenment. He felt he understood the basic truths about life and knew how to escape from this earthly existence and the law of karma. He had become the Buddha – the enlightened one.

Through this profound experience called *Bodhi* ("awakening"), Gautama believed he now understood the nature of suffering, both its cause and a way of stopping it.

"I have run through the course of many births looking for the maker of this dwelling and finding him not; repeated birth is painful. Now you are seen, O builder of the house, you will not build the house again. All your rafters are broken, your ridge-pole is destroyed, the mind, set on the attainment of nirvana, has attained the extinction of desires." *Dhammapuda 153-54, dating from when Gautama received the light of illumination*

Itinerant teaching
Buddha spent the rest of his life teaching the way that leads to the end of suffering. Accompanied by a growing group of followers he traveled throughout India preaching sermons based on his Four Noble Truths and the Middle Path.

His death
Buddha died (c. 486 BCE) at the age of 80 in the town of Kushinagara, India.

By then he had a considerable following and a well-organized community.

His followers believe that on his death Buddha entered into the blissful state of *Nirvana* where he is free from all suffering.

Buddha's break with Hinduism
Buddha did more than merely adapt Hinduism – he taught a new religion.

Similarities

- Both religions believe in reincarnation.
- Both religions believe in the law of *karma*.

Differences

- Buddha rejected the idea that the *atman* (individual soul) had to be united with Brahman (the source of the world). Buddhists believe that the idea of the annihilation of the self is a Hindu heresy.
- Buddha did not adopt the Hindu sacred writings.
- Buddha rejected the caste system.
- Buddha did not accept the idea of the existence of God in the sense that he was a higher being.

Beliefs of Buddhism

God
Buddhism does not believe in an omnipotent, creator God who exists apart from our universe. Buddhists do not worship Buddha.

Karma
Karma, the moral law of cause and effect, is active in both the moral and physical realms. This law states that each action has a consequence for one's future happiness or unhappiness.

Dukkha
Buddhism teaches that all existence is *dukkha*, that is, it has no permanence.

Dukkha is both the impermanence and the suffering that results from it.

Nirvana
Nirvana is the state of enlightenment in which all action and interaction cease.

The form in which one is reborn, animal or human, in heaven or in hell, depends on the ethical law of *karma*. But one escapes from this endless cycle when one attains *nirvana*.

Ways to gain merit
Only Buddhist nuns and monks expect to gain *nirvana* when they die. Buddhists believe that by doing many good deeds they will have a better existence in the next life. These good deeds include:

- supporting monasteries;
- making pilgrimages to Buddhist shrines;
- giving food to monks and nuns;
- doing good deeds to other people;
- building a memorial to Buddha.

Shwe Dagon, Rangoon, one of the most famous of the Buddhist pagodas, has most impressive golden spires. In order to gain merit, Buddhists give gold leaf to the temple so that the gold on the spires may be constantly renewed.

The Five Precepts
In everyday life all Buddhists aim to follow the Five Precepts. These act as positive ethical restraints on Buddhists and provide a set of guidelines to follow.

1. Do not harm or kill any living thing.
2. Do not steal or take anything that is not given to you.
3. Do not indulge in any wrong sexual relations.
4. Do not lie or speak in an unkind way to anyone.
5. Do not drink alcohol or take drugs.

The Three Jewels of Buddhism
The Three Jewels of Buddhism, also called the "Three Refuges of Buddhism," supposedly given by Buddha himself, are a dedication used by Buddhists. The words are treasured by Buddhists because of the support that they give.

- I take refuge in Buddha.
- I take refuge in *dhamma* (holy writings).
- I take refuge in *sangha* (monks and nuns).

Monks and the Dalai Lama

Monks in Buddha's day

Buddha founded an order of monks who had to follow severe rules of discipline:

1. Dress in rags.
2. Over the rags wear a yellow cloak.
3. Eat only once a day.
4. Never handle money.
5. Possess nothing that is not given in the begging bowls.
6. For part of the year live under a tree in a forest.

Ignoring the prevailing Hindu caste system, Buddha allowed merchants as well as Brahmins into his community of monks.

In the beginning Buddha did not allow women into the order, but later his stepmother persuaded him to admit women.

Buddhist monks and nuns today

Buddhist monks and nuns do not have to follow such an austere set of rules and they live in monasteries rather than the open air. However, following the example of Buddha, who depended entirely on other people's charity, they live simple lives engaged in the study of their sacred texts and in meditation. They can own:

- a begging-bowl
- a needle
- a razor
- a water filter
- three robes.

The Dalai Lama

The *Gelukpa* ("Yellow Hat") monks of
Tibet have the Dalai Lama (the chief of
the lamas) as their leader.

Lama is Tibetan for "spiritual leader."
Dalai is Mongolian for "ocean." Hence,
Dalai Lama is translated as "ocean of
wisdom."

Like his predecessors, Tenzin Gyatso,
who is the present and fourteenth
Dalai Lama, is believed to be the
incarnation of the *Bodhisattva
Avalokiteshvara.*

"For as long as space endures and for
as long as living beings remain, until
then may I, too, abide to dispel the
misery of the world." *The Dalai Lama*

Exile

The present Dalai Lama was born in
1935 in Tibet but, since 1959, when the
Chinese army invaded Tibet, he has
lived in exile in Dharamsala, India.
Today, he travels the world teaching and
explaining the plight of Tibetan
Buddhists.

Nobel Peace Prize

In 1989 the Dalai Lama was awarded the
Nobel Peace Prize.

"Establishing binding ethical
principles is possible when we take as
our starting point the observation that
we all desire happiness and wish to
avoid suffering." *From the Nobel Lecture
delivered by the Dalai Lama on December 11,
1989, the day after receiving the Nobel Peace
Prize, at Aula, Oslo's University*

Holy books of Buddhism

When Buddha was alive his teachings were memorized by his followers and at his death were passed on by word of mouth.

In 253 BCE, nearly 200 years after Buddha's death, a synod was held at Pataliputta (the third Buddhist synod). At this synod Buddhist traditions were clarified, checked and agreed upon.

They were not, however, written down until the first century CE. This was done in Ceylon and resulted in the Pali canon.

The triple basket (*Tripitaka*)

The Pali canon is known as the "triple basket" or *Tripitaka* because it has three parts which were originally written out on palm leaves and stored in a basket.

1. *Vinaya-Pitaka*

The first part, *Vinaya-Pitaka*, is called the "basket of order." It contains:

- a short biography of Buddha;
- a record of his first monastic community;
- his rules by which his monastery was governed:
  a. to live peacefully
  b. to care for the ill
  c. to give to charity
  d. teachers and pupils must receive instruction;
- a detailed explanation of the Public Confession (*uposatha*);
- rules concerning ceremonies.

THE WISE MAN

Should one see a wise man, who, like a revealer of treasure, points out faults and reproves; let one associate with such a wise person; it will be better, not worse, for him who associates with such a one.

Let him advise, instruct, and dissuade one from evil; truly pleasing is he to the good, displeasing is he to the bad.

Associate not with evil friends, associate not with mean men; associate with good friends, associate with noble men.

He who practises the Dhamma abides in happiness with mind pacified; the wise man ever delights in the Dhamma revealed by the Ariyas.

Irrigators lead the water; fletchers fashion the shaft; carpenters carve the wood; the wise discipline themselves.

As a solid rock is not shaken by the wind, even so the wise remain unshaken amidst blame and praise.

Just as a deep lake is clear and still, even so, on hearing the teachings, the wise become exceedingly peaceful.

The good give up (attachment for) everything; the saintly prattle not with sensual craving; whether affected by happiness or by pain, the wise show neither elation nor depression.

Neither for the sake of oneself nor for the sake of another (does a wise person do any wrong); he should not desire son, wealth, or kingdom (by doing wrong); by unjust means he should not seek his own success. Then (only) such a one is indeed virtuous, wise and righteous.

Few among men are they who cross to the further shore. The other folk only run up and down the bank on this side.

But those who act rightly according to the teaching, which is well expounded, those are they who will reach the Beyond-Nivana (crossing) the realm of passions, so hard to cross.

A wise man renounces evil and sensual pleasure and he does all meritorious work in order to attain Nivana. He becomes a homeless one.

By having no attachment and desires and by forsaking sensual pleasures, a wise man gets rid of his impurities.

Those, who practice the seven Factors (Mindfulness, Investigation of the Dhamma, Energy, Rapture, Calmness, Concentration, Equanimity), and have freed themselves from attachments, attain Nivana. *Dhammapada, Panditavagga, The Wise Man, verses 76-89*

2. Sutta-Pitaka

The second part, the *Sutta-Pitaka*, is an instruction book. It contains the teachings of Buddha and his monks as well as 547 stories from Buddha's previous incarnations.

The *Sutta-Pitaka* also has one of the best known texts of the Pali canon, the *Dhammapada*, consisting of 26 chapters (423 verses) of sayings of Buddha.

3. Abhidhamma-Pitaka

The third part, the *Abhidhamma-Pitaka*, the "basket of higher teaching," consists of seven books of advanced, academic Buddhist teaching.

The Four Noble Truths and the Eightfold Path

The Four Noble Truths

After Buddha had reached the Deer Park in Benares he preached his first sermon setting out the following principles that later became known as the Four Noble Truths – the key beliefs and values of Buddhism.

1. The fact of suffering

We suffer at birth, throughout our lives and at death. Human life is full of suffering and is therefore evil.

2. The cause of suffering

Greed is the cause of human suffering.

3. The remedy for suffering

If we could ever manage to cease from desire our suffering would end. This is the aim of Buddhism. *Nirvana* (literally "a blowing-out") extinguishes once and for all the flame of desire.

4. The escape from suffering

Release from suffering comes by following the Eightfold Path.

The Eightfold Path

Buddha taught that the Eightfold Path, or the Middle Path, lay between the path of extreme hardship and the path of extreme luxury. He had tasted the path of luxury and the path of yoga and found no satisfaction in either.

To become more compassionate and wise and to escape from suffering the following eight steps must be taken:

- Right understanding
- Right thinking
- Right speaking
- Right acting
- Right lifestyle
- Right endeavoring
- Right mindfulness
- Right contemplation.

1. Step one: right understanding

This is achieved by understanding Buddha's teaching, in particular the Four Noble Truths.

This will give a right understanding of the world.

2. Step two: right thinking

This means having the correct attitude toward the Middle Path.

3. Step three: right speaking

Buddhists are not to lie, slander other people or boast about themselves.

They must avoid any kind of offensive speech.

4. Step four: right acting

This relates to conduct. Buddhists are always to behave in moral ways. They must never steal and must always be kind and compassionate to people and to all living creatures.

Buddha said, "Let a man overcome evil by good."

5. Step five: right lifestyle (occupation)

This means refusing any work which

involves selling alcohol, causing bloodshed, or slave-trading.

6. Step six: right effort, or endeavor

This means concentrating on things which are good and tranquil. All kinds of evil are to be rejected. Truth is to be sought and followed.

7. Step seven: right mindfulness

Buddhists are always to think before they speak. They must seek to be free from any unnecessary desire and from extremes of self-indulgence and self-denial.

The five "hindrances" from which they must seek to be free are:

- covetousness
- malevolence
- sloth
- worry
- doubt.

8. Step eight: right contemplation/meditation

Full concentration is required, for it is contemplation that leads to *nirvana*.

There are seven steps to take to achieve this awakening:

- mindfulness through investigating *dhamma*
- have a pure mental state
- energy
- rapture of mind
- impassibility of the body
- concentration
- even-mindedness.

Buddhist symbols

The wheel of life

Buddhists believe that many states of rebirth must be undergone before *nirvana* is reached.

The wheel of life symbolizes Buddha's teaching. The circular form of this wheel symbolizes the ceaseless worldly existence. The wheel is held by the claws and teeth of a monster, signifying the state of mind that passionately clings to this world. The hub of the wheel contains three animals:

- the rooster – signifying desire or lust;
- the snake – signifying anger;

- the pig – symbolizing ignorance and stupidity.

These are at the center of the wheel because they are the root cause of earth's troubles.

Eight lucky signs

These Buddhist symbols are sometimes referred to as "The Eight Auspicious Symbols."

1. The parasol (*dug*)

The parasol symbolizes the authority of Buddha. As the parasol protects the head from the sun so Buddha's teaching protects the mind from scorching passion and all other evils.

2. The vase (*bhumpa*)

This treasure vase represents a repository of limitless material wealth, good health and long life.

3. The conch shell (*dhungkar*)

The white conch shell which coils to the right symbolizes the deep, far-reaching, reverberating and melodious sound of *dharma* teachings. It signifies an awakening from the slumber of ignorance and is a call to travel on the path of noble deeds that benefit other people.

Gautama blew the conch shell when he preached the law. Today, in memory of this, the conch shell is blown whenever an important lama preaches a special sermon.

4. The victory banner (*gyaltsen*)

This symbol used in processions signifies, in general, the victory of piety and goodness over evil forces; and, in particular, the complete victory of Buddhist teaching over all harmful forces.

5. A pair of golden fish (*sernya*)

These fish symbolize rebirth and resurrection to eternal life. The golden fish symbolize living beings in a state of fearlessness without danger of drowning in the ocean of sufferings. They are able to migrate from place to place spontaneously just as fish swim freely and fearlessly through water.

6. The lotus flower (*pema*)

The lotus flower symbolizes the ultimate goal of enlightenment. As the lotus comes out of mud but does not carry any dirt, so Buddhist teaching is free of all earthly concerns. According to the Lalitavistara, "The spirit of the best of men is spotless, like the new lotus in the [muddy] water which does not adhere to it."

7. Knot of eternity (*palbheu*)

This symbolizes Buddha's teaching which has no beginning and no end.

8. The wheel of *dharma* (*choekyi khorlo*)

This golden wheel symbolizes the propagation of Buddha's teaching. Buddha's first sermon, which set in motion the cycle of law, is symbolized by the wheel's eight spokes which stand for the noble eightfold path.

In Indian art these wheels were often placed on four lions standing back to back and facing the four cardinal points.

Footprints of the Buddha (*buddhapada*)

The footprints of the Buddha are venerated in all Buddhist countries. The footprints, cut out of stone, are highly schematized. All the toes are usually of equal length. The footprints often include distinguishing marks like a *dharma* wheel engraved or painted on the sole.

Buddhist worship

Shrines

Strictly speaking there is no worship since Buddhists do not believe in a god. They simply visit temples and shrines to pay their respects to Buddha and to meditate.

In Buddhist temples the image of Buddha is always placed in the main part of the building which becomes his shrine. Devout Buddhists sit barefoot opposite the statue. They pay homage to Buddha by intoning the Three Refuges and the Five Precepts.

The 108 beads of a *seikbadi* (akin to a rosary) may be used. Buddha's name is said as each bead passes through the fingers.

Stupas and pagodas
Stupas (dome-shaped memorial shrines)

After Buddha died he was cremated and his ashes were divided and sent to the different provinces in which he had preached. The first Buddhist shrines consisted of ten mounds (stupas) built of stone. They were erected to house these ashes.

Other stupas were built either for important Buddhist monks or to house relics of Buddha. If no relic was available, stupas were built over copies of sacred Buddhist books. Over the centuries these stupas became increasingly elaborate.

Today, stupas usually form part of a Buddhist temple complex.

Pagodas

Buddhist pagodas (many-storied, tapering towers) are erected as memorials or shrines. They are usually five-storied, made of wood, with superb carpentry.

The five-tiered roofs stand for the five basic elements of the universe: earth, water, fire, wind and emptiness while spires on the roof symbolize wisdom.

Pilgrimages

The most important places of pilgrimage for Buddhists are all closely linked to Buddha himself.

Devout Buddhists are keen to make pilgrimages to four places:

- to Kapilavastu, Buddha's birthplace;
- to Bodh Gaya where Buddha was enlightened;
- to Benares where Buddha preached his first sermon;
- to Kusinara where Buddha died.

Other places of pilgrimage

For the Buddhist, places where relics of Buddha are buried are sacred places of pilgrimage. The chief ones are:

- Borobordur, in Java where a branch of Buddha's bodhi tree is planted;
- Rangoon, at the Golden Pagoda, also known as Shwe Dagon, where a relic of Buddha's hair is buried;
- Kandy, in Sri Lanka, at the Temple of the Sacred Tooth.

Festivals

Buddhist festivals are closely associated with incidents in Buddha's life.

Different countries hold different Buddhist festivals.

Asala Puja, "Day of Proclamation"

This celebrates Buddha's first sermon and is held on the first full moon in July.

Hana Matsuri: "The Festival of Flowers" (Japan)

This commemorates an event in Buddha's childhood when in the park of Lumbini he was bathed in a sweet-scented lake. During such festivals Buddha's statue may be washed with such things as hydrangea leaves and sweet tea. An image of Buddha, decked in a garland of flowers, is paraded through streets which are strewn with paper lotus flowers.

Advantages of a pilgrimage

Buddhists are taught that making a pilgrimage brings them:

- merit
- blessing
- greater spiritual understanding
- rebirth into a better life.

Buddhist "schools" (movements) and Zen Buddhism

Buddhist groups

After Buddha died his followers formed different schools centered on differing interpretations of his teaching. Today there are many schools and practices. The chief ones are:

1. The *Theravada* School

The Theravada School, with over 100 million followers, reached as far as:

- Sri Lanka
- Burma
- Thailand
- Cambodia
- Laos.

The *Theravada*, or Southern Buddhism, has its scriptures preserved in Pali, an ancient Indian language closely related to Sanskrit. Of the three major schools of Buddhism, *Theravada* sticks more closely to the beliefs and practices of the ancient Buddhism of India.

Theravada Buddhists believe that Buddha entered into *nirvana* the moment he died and that he himself is not able to help anyone himself today. Salvation must, therefore, be attained solely through one's own efforts.

2. The *Mahayana* School

The *Mahayana* School, or, Eastern/ Northern Buddhism, has its scriptures preserved in Chinese.

Mahayana Buddhists believe that Buddha did not achieve *nirvana* in his own lifetime because he spent his life teaching others so all who call on him today will be helped by his spirit.

The *Mahayana* School is a very diverse school and has managed to co-exist with Confucianism, Taoism, Shinto and Communism. It is found in:

- Nepal
- Korea
- China
- Japan
- Vietnam.

3. The *Vajrayana* School

The *Vajrayana* School of Buddhism, is also known as Tibetan or Northern Buddhism as its scriptures are preserved in Tibetan. The *Vajrayana* School spread to:

- Tibet
- Bhutan
- Mongolia.

Zen Buddhism

Japan

Buddhism was brought to Japan in about 550 CE by Buddhist monks who traveled from China and Korea.

All Japanese Buddhists belong to the *Mahayana* School of Buddhism but have a wide variety of practices.

Perhaps the best-known group is Zen ("meditation") which teaches that the truth is to be found in a person's own heart and may be known by meditation and self-mastery.

Zen masters

Zen Buddhism derives is practices from two leading Buddhist teachers:

- Eisai, 1141–1215
- Dogen, 1200–1253.

They both introduced new ideas about meditation, helping their disciples to meditate in such a way that they controlled their minds and achieved an inner stillness.

Riddles

A *koan* (a paradoxical statement or puzzling question) was an exercise used by Eisai when teaching novices. The attempt to understand or solve the *koan* opened the mind to receiving new understanding of Zen on an intuitive level.

One such riddle said,

"When both hands are clapped a sound is produced. Listen to the sound of one hand clapping."

Zen monasteries

Many Zen monasteries have sand gardens. Their rocks and raked sand are laid out to represent ocean waves or mountains.

Zen monks and nuns engage in meditation and work in their monasteries. Their few possessions include:

- a conical straw hat, to give protection from the sun
- a pair of wicker sandals
- a black robe
- a cloth bag in which they collect alms.

Meditation

Meditation forms the core of Zen Buddhism.

In this focused way Zen Buddhists were led into a state of enlightenment or spiritual awakening. The purposes of Zen meditation are to achieve greater self-awareness and to enter a state of enlightenment. Aids to meditation:

- sitting beside or tending the sand gardens;
- martial arts (sports such as archery and karate which teach mental and physical control require a great deal of concentration);
- meditation on *haikus*. *Haikus* are Japanese lyric verses with three unrhymed lines of 5, 5 and 7 syllables. Traditionally they invoke the seasons or an aspect of nature.

F.A.Qs (Frequently Asked Questions) about Buddhism

Q: Why do some statues of Buddha show him lying on his side?
A: This is the posture in which Buddha died.

Q: Why is the lotus plant important in Buddhism?
A: It is a symbol of Buddhism. As the lotus flower follows the sun, so Buddhists are to follow knowledge.

Q: Why do Zen monks and nuns shave their heads?
A: As a symbol that they have given up their worldly lives.

Q: Are Buddhists out to convert the world?
A: Buddhism does not actively look for converts and easily co-exists with other faiths. It does, however, welcome those who do want to convert.

Q: What insight characterizes Buddhism?
A: Buddhists believe that there is nothing that permanently exists.

Q: Does Buddhism have a flag?
A: The Buddhist flag is a modern creation, jointly designed by J. R. de Silva and Colonel Henry S. Olcott to mark the revival of Buddhism in Ceylon in 1880.

The World Buddhist Congress of 1952 accepted it as the International Buddhist flag.

Colonel Olcott designed a flag from the six colors of the aura that he believed shone around the head of the Buddha after his enlightenment.

The first five stripes of the flag have five colors:

Color	Symbol for
• Blue	Universal compassion
• Yellow	The Middle Path
• Red	Blessings
• White	Purity and liberation
• Orange	Wisdom.

5 SIKHISM

Introduction

"Sikh," a Hindi word, comes originally from the Sanskrit word for "disciple." Sikhs are disciples of the gurus (teachers).

Sikhism originated 500 years ago in the Punjab, the "land of the five rivers," in north-west India. It sprang from the teaching of Guru Nanak who, seeing that many people felt excluded from India's two dominant religions, Hinduism and Islam, preached a simple message of: devotion, remembrance of God at all times, truthful living and the equality of humankind.

The teachings of Sikhism's ten gurus are enshrined in the Sikh holy book – *Guru Granth Sahib*.

Origins of Sikhism

Nanak

Nanak was born at Talwandi, India into the Hindu warrior class or caste (*kshatriya*). As a young man he would get up before dawn to bathe in the river and meditate. One morning he fell into a deep trance lasting three days. In the trance he was taken to God's court and given heavenly nectar to drink.

The day after Nanak woke from the trance, he proclaimed, "There is no Hindu or Muslim." From then on he began to teach that the only satisfactory way to find God was to search for him in one's heart.

For the next 21 years Nanak preached throughout India gaining many followers from among both Hindus and Muslims. He also embarked on missionary journeys to Sri Lanka, Baghdad and Mecca.

A spiritual succession

Determined that there should be a spiritual rather than a physical succession of his teaching after he died, Nanak did not appoint any member of his family to succeed him. Instead he chose Bhai Lehna to whom he gave the name "Angad," derived from the word ang, meaning "limb." The name was an indication of Nanak's wish that the next guru would be an extension of himself. Bhai Lehna was the first of nine further gurus.

The Sikh gurus

Sikhism has a specific definition for the word "guru." It means the descent of divine guidance to humankind through ten Enlightened Masters. As the gurus were thought to be perfect, it was taught that they were not reborn under the law of *karma* but returned to this earth as God's messengers through whom he revealed himself.

The divine spirit was passed from one Guru to the next as "the light of a lamp which lights another does not abate." Similarly, a spiritual leader and his disciple became equal. The gurus were revered but were never worshiped because worship was offered to God alone. Gurus are still held in high esteem and pictures of them are often seen in Sikh temples and homes.

The religion of the gurus

The ten Sikh gurus lived from 1469 to 1708 CE in northern India. Even though they only came from the warrior caste of Hinduism (*kshatriya*) they became the teachers of the Sikh faith. Their qualification for being a Sikh guru came from the fact that they received their revelation straight from God.

The ten Sikh gurus

- Guru Nanak, 1469–1539
- Guru Angad, 1539–52
- Guru Amar Das, 1552–74
- Guru Ram Das, 1574–81
- Guru Arjan, 1581–1606
- Guru Har Gobind, 1606–44
- Guru Har Rai1, 1644–61
- Guru Har Krishan, 1661–64
- Guru Tegh Bahadur, 1664–75
- Guru Gobind Singh, 1675–1708

Sikh scriptures

Inspired texts

The Sikh scriptures may not be the actual words of God, but Sikhs still believe that they are divinely inspired.

These scriptures are the embodiment of the Sikh guru and are given as much respect as a human guru. Today, it is these scriptures, rather than any living person, that are the true spiritual authority of the Sikh religion.

Adi Granth

The principle Sikh scripture is the *Adi Granth* (often referred to as the *Guru Granth Sahib*).

Adi Granth means "first collection or compilation." They are written in Gurmukhi, a script for writing Punjabi and they contain:

- 974 of Guru Nanak's poems and hymns
- writings of six other gurus
- writings of 12 non-Sikhs.

The centrality of the scriptures

In this collection of devotional hymns and poetry it is stressed that Sikhs should meditate on the true Guru (God). The scriptures provide moral and ethical rules and give teaching on the way of spiritual salvation and unity with God.

Showing respect for the Sikh scriptures

Sikhism rejects idol worship and therefore *Guru Granth Sahib* is not worshiped, though it is held in great respect. This is shown in many ways:

THE INFINITE VALUE OF GURU GRANTH SAHIB

"The Palace of the Lord God is so beautiful. Within it, there are gems, rubies, pearls and flawless diamonds. A fortress of gold surrounds this Source of Nectar. How can I climb up to the Fortress without a ladder? By meditating on the Lord, through the Guru, I am blessed and exalted. The Guru is the Ladder, the Guru is the Boat, and the Guru is the Raft to take me to the Lord's Name. The Guru is the Boat to carry me across the world-ocean; the Guru is the Sacred Shrine of Pilgrimage, the Guru is the Holy River. If it pleases Him, I bathe in the Pool of Truth, and become radiant and pure." *Guru Nanak, Sri Rag, pg. 17*

Every morning Sikhs recite the following:

"There exists but one God, who is called the True, the Creator. He is free from fear and hate, immortal, not begotten, self-existent, great and compassionate. The True was at the beginning, the True was at the distant part. The True is at the present, O Nanak, the True will be also in the future." *Guru Nanak, Adi Granth*

- when not in use it is covered with a *romalla*, a silk cloth;
- it rests on a special platform or dais;
- Sikh worshipers prostrate themselves before the *Guru Granth Sahib* on entering the temple;
- throughout their time in the *gurdwara* (temple) worshipers sit on the floor, emphasizing the unique status given to *Guru Granth Sahib* as it is raised up on its throne;

- they leave offerings next to it before they leave the temple;
- no shoes are allowed to be worn in its presence;
- one must never turn one's back to it.

Granthi

Sikhs do not have any priests, but most Sikh temples have a reader (*granthi*) who reads the Sikh scriptures. A *granthi* can be a man or a woman and is chosen from among devout Sikh worshipers.

Sikh worship

Gurdwara (temple)

A Sikh temple (*gurdwara*, meaning "the guru's door" or "God's house") can be simply a room in which there is a copy of the Sikh scriptures (*the Guru Granth Sahib*).

Sikh *shabads* (hymns), form the central part of Sikh worship.

The Sikh emblem

Every *gurdwara* displays a flag bearing the Sikh emblem. It comprises three symbols, each representing an important Sikh belief about God. These three symbols are:

1. The *khanda*

This double-edged sword indicates that Sikhs will fight for God's truth, with force if necessary. The sword also stands for the supreme truth, that is, the one God.

2. The *chakra*

A chakra or circle is laid over the blade of the *khanda*. As a circle has no beginning or end so the *chakra* stands for God's infinity.

The circle also reminds Sikhs that they are totally united to the one God.

3. Two *kirpans*

The outside of the Sikh symbol consists of a pair of kirpans (scimitar-like cutting swords). They stand for the power of the Sikh gurus. The swords stand for both:

- spiritual power (*peeri*)
- political power (*meeri*)

These swords remind Sikhs that it is their duty to defend the truth.

Worship in a *gurdwara*

When Sikhs enter their temples they take off their shoes and cover their heads. The worship is comprised of four elements:

- *Kirtan*: singing hymns from the *Guru Granth Sahib*;
- *Sahib*: readings from the *Guru Granth Sahib* (sometimes with an explanation);
- prayers: these always end with a set prayer called *ardas* (for which everyone stands);
- the sharing of *karah prasad*: an offering of semolina, water and butter.

Langar

At the end of the time of worship a complete meal is served in the dining part of the *gurdwara*. This *langar* (free community kitchen) has been a feature of Sikh living since the days of Guru Nanak. Every *gurdwara* has a *langar* and it is open not only for the Sikhs who have just been worshiping, but to all visitors of all religions.

Sikh shrines: the Golden Temple

The Sikh's oldest and most sacred shrine is the *Harimandir Sahib* ("Temple of God"). It is commonly known as the Golden Temple or *Darbar Sahib* ("Divine Court"). It is found in the city of Amritsar, Punjab.

Today's building stands on a holy lake, *Amritsar* ("The Pool of Nectar"), where Guru Nanak used to meditate. Completed in 1766, it is magnificently decorated with gold-leaf and copper-gilt inscriptions from the *Guru Granth Sahib*.

Sikhs are not specifically required to make pilgrimages, because all places where *Guru Granth Sahib* are installed are considered equally holy for Sikhs. Most, however, do visit the Golden Temple as it is a living symbol of the spiritual and historical traditions of the Sikhs. It is a source of inspiration for all Sikhs and their chief place of pilgrimage.

The *Harimandir Sahib* has entrances

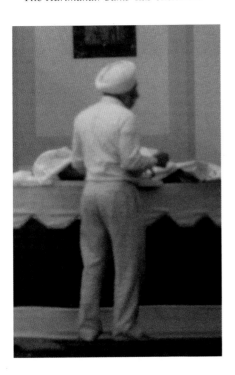

and doors on all four sides. Guru Arjun Dev once explained: "My faith is for the people of all castes and all creeds from whichever direction they come and to whichever direction they bow."

1984

In early June 1984 the Indian Army invaded the Golden Temple complex to apprehend Sant Jarnail Singh Bhindranwale, a Sikh militant leader.

The sacred sanctity of the Golden Temple complex was violated and desecrated in the most brutal and unholy way. Thousands of innocent visiting pilgrims and temple workers were killed, the Sikh library with precious manuscripts of the gurus was burned to the ground, and the continuous reading of *Sri Guru Granth Sahib* in *Harmandir Sahib* was interrupted for the first time in hundreds of years.

The destruction and loss of life marked the darkest chapter in Sikh history in the twentieth century. Restoration work took 15 years to complete.

Indira Gandhi's assassination

In October 1984 Indira Gandhi was assassinated by two of her own bodyguards – Shahid Beant Singh and Shahid Satwant Singh Ji. Both were Sikhs. Shahid Beant Singh was killed on the spot, while Satwant Singh was convicted and hung later. Both are now revered as Sikh martyrs.

Sikh ceremonies and festivals

Nam Karan

Nam Karan celebrates the birth and naming of a baby. In a *gurdwara* appropriate hymns of joy from the *Guru Granth Sahib* are recited.

A *karah prashad* (sacred pudding) is prepared by the family, and *amrit* (sweet water) is given to the infant and the mother.

The young child's name is chosen when the *granthi* (reader) randomly opens *Guru Granth Sahib* and reads the hymn from that page. The child's name must start with the first letter of the first word of that hymn. The name is chosen and then announced to the congregation.

Amrit Sanskar (baptism)

This ceremony initiates a Sikh into the *Khalsa* brotherhood (see page 116).

Marriages

During the ceremony the bride follows the bridegroom as he walks four times round the dais on which the *Guru Granth Sahib* rests.

Funerals

Sikhs view death as a natural process in line with God's will. Public displays of grief at funerals are discouraged and deemed inappropriate.

All Sikhs are cremated. As the body is being burnt, *Kirtan Sohila*, a night-time prayer, is recited and *Ardas* is prayed. The ashes are immersed in the nearest river.

There is a period of mourning lasting ten days and during this time the whole of the *Guru Granth Sahib* is read aloud.

Akhand path

The non-stop reading of the *Guru Granth Sahib* from cover to cover is called *akhand path*. It takes places in times of hardship, but especially at times of celebration, such as birth, marriage, death or moving into a new home. It takes about 48 hours to read.

Gurpurbs

Gurpurbs are important anniversaries linked to the lives of the gurus. The most important are:

- first installation of Sri Guru Granth Sahib in the Golden Temple by Guru Arjan Dev;
- birth of Guru Nanak (traditionally celebrated in November);
- birth of Guru Gobind Singh;
- martyrdom of Guru Arjan Dev;
- martyrdom of Guru Tegh Bahadur;
- martyrdom of the Sahibzadas (the sons of Guru Gobind Singh).

Baisakhji (April 13)

Baisakhji celebrates the Sikh new year and the birthday of the *Khalsa* order (see page 116).

Sikhs visit *gurdwaras* where special devotions are held. During the celebration the Sikh flag (*nishan sahib*) and the cloth around the flag pole are ceremonially renewed.

Fairs and processions are also times of

celebration, the best-known being a large animal fair at Amritsar.

Divali

Guru Amar Das founded this special day of celebration when he ordered all Sikhs to meet at Goindwal to receive blessings from the gurus.

In 1577 the foundation stone of the Golden Temple was laid on *Divali*.

On *Divali* 1619 the Golden Temple was illuminated with lights to welcome home and celebrate the release of Guru Hargobind from imprisonment in Gwalior fort.

Divali continues to be a festival of lights when candles and *devas* (lamps) decorate the outside of *gurdwaras*.

Hola Mohalla

Guru Gobind Singh started this festival when he collected the *Khalsa* Sikhs at Anandpur on the day following the Indian festival of Holi. Dividing them into two armies he held military exercises and mock battles. These were followed by music and poetry competitions. Anandpur is still the biggest center for the annual celebration of this festival.

Sikh beliefs

Sikh beliefs

God created life. The divine spark is in
everyone. Everyone has to go through
the cycle of reincarnation, that is, rebirth
after death. It is impossible to break free
from this cycle without God's help. All
actions are important, because the way
people live now determines the type of
life they will have in the next
incarnation. Each person has free will to
follow God or to reject his way.

God

- God is one.
- God is the truth.
- God is eternal.
- God is the creator and sustainer of
  all life.
- God has no shape, no gender, no
  incarnations (earthly forms).
- God has revealed himself to
  humankind through the teachings
  conveyed by the gurus.

Simran and seva

Simran is the name given to the
awareness of God and to meditation
about him.

Seva refers to serving others in the
community without expecting anything
in return.

Equality

In the eyes of God everyone is equal. To
show this Sikh men and women take
one particular name each:

- Singh (lion) is the surname taken by
  Sikh men.

- Kaur (princess) is the surname taken
  by Sikh women.

Features of Sikh communities

1. Equality

There is no caste system in Sikhism
because all people are equal in God's
eyes.

2. Morality

Sikhs promote tolerance and truthfulness and oppose adultery and gambling.

5. Giving money

Sikhs donate 10% of their income to their own community or to charity.

6. Other faiths

Other faiths are not only tolerated, but viewed very sympathetically. Sikhs do not believe that they have a monopoly on the truth but hold that Sikhism is one way to God out of many possible ways.

7. No clergy

Sikhs believe that each person has direct access to God and therefore, they have no need for priests.

Sikh Code of Conduct

- one Immortal Being;
- ten gurus, from Guru Nanak Dev to Guru Gobind Singh;
- the *Guru Granth Sahib* (the scriptures);
- the utterances and teachings of the ten gurus;
- the baptism bequeathed by the tenth guru;
- allegiance to no other religion.

Sikhs are those who hold on to this Code of Conduct.

"Without the Code of Conduct, One can not be referred to as a 'Sikh'. Without the Code of Conduct, One will suffer in the Lord's Court."
Rahit Nama Bhai Desa Singh Ji

3. Good deeds

Sikhs believe that as they do good to others they are drawn closer to God.

4. Service

Sikhs encourage hard work. All work is seen as a vocation. They believe that it is preferable to live in the world and work for its welfare than to withdraw from it and become an ascetic. However, Nanak taught his followers to live self-disciplined lives.

The words of the gurus

The quest for truth

"Realization of Truth is higher than all else.
Higher still is Truthful Living."
Guru Nanak, Sri Rag

There is only one God, the Creator

"You are the Creator, O Lord, the Unknowable. You created the Universe of diverse kinds, colors and qualities. You know your own Creation. All this is your Play." *Guru Nanak, Var Majh*

God is not revealed in any incarnations

"He [God] neither has father, nor mother, nor sons nor brothers."
Guru Nanak, Maru

"Burnt be the mouth that asserts the Lord takes birth. He is neither born nor dies; neither enters birth nor departs." *Guru Arjan Dev, Raga Bhairon*

Five cardinal vices

The five cardinal vices are:

- *kam* (lust)
- *krodh* (anger)
- *lobh* (greed)
- *moh* (worldly attachment)
- *ahankar* (pride).

Salvation is achieved by overcoming them.

"Five thieves who live within this body are lust, anger, greed, attachment and ego. They rob us of ambrosia, but the egocentrics do not understand it and no one listens to their cries." *Guru Amar Das, Sorath*

"I am in the Refuge of the Lord; Bless me, O Lord with your Grace, so that the lust, anger, greed, attachment and ego may be destroyed." *Guru Arjan Dev, Gauri Sukhmani*

Empty rituals are to be rejected
Blind rituals such as fasting, religious vegetarianism, pilgrimages, superstitions, yoga, as well as any form of idol worship should not be indulged in.

"Let good conduct be thy fasting."
Guru Nanak, Var Majh

"Only fools argue whether to eat meat or not. They don't understand truth nor do they meditate on it. Who can define what is meat and what is plant? Who knows where the sin lies, being a vegetarian or a non-vegetarian?" *Guru Nanak, Var Malar*

"Whosover controls the mind, he is a pilgrim." *Guru Arjan Dev, Maru Solhe*

"The way to true yoga is found by dwelling in God and remaining detached in the midst of worldly attachments." *Guru Nanak, Suhi*

Equality of creed, race and sex

"All are created from the seed of God. There is the same clay in the whole world, the potter [God] makes many kinds of pots." *Guru Amar Das, Bhairo*

Sikhs reject the caste system

"Recognize the light of God and do not ask for the caste. There is no caste in the next world." *Guru Nanak, Asa*

Sikhs affirm that women should be treated as well as men
Sikhs reject:

- female infanticide
- *sati* (wife burning)
- *purdah* (women wearing veils)
- forcing widows never to remarry.

"We are born of woman, we are conceived in the womb of woman, we are engaged and married to woman. We make friendship with woman and

the lineage continued because of woman. When one woman dies, we take another one, we are bound with the world through woman. Why should we talk ill of her, who gives birth to kings? The woman is born from woman; there is none without her. Only the One True Lord is without woman." *Guru Nanak, Var Asa*

"They cannot be called satis, who burn themselves with their dead husbands. They can only be called satis, if they bear the shock of separation. They may also be known as satis, who live with character and contentment and always show veneration to their husbands by remembering them." *Guru Amar Das, Var Suhi*

Honest labor and work, *kirat karna,* is an honorable way to earn one's living, but begging is not

"He who eats what he earns through his earnest labor and from his hand gives something in charity; he alone, O Nanak, knows the true way of life." *Guru Nanak Dev, Rag Sarang, pg. 1245*

The five Ks and F.A.Qs about Sikhism

The *Khalsa*

The origins of the *Khalsa*, an especially devout and committed community of Sikhs, dates back to 1699 CE. Guru Gobind Singh challenged a group of his followers to volunteer themselves as human sacrifices. He did this by standing in front of his tent, sword in hand, asking if any of them would lay down their lives for their guru. One man came forward and he was taken into Guru Gobind's tent. Only the guru came out of the tent, with his sword dripping with blood. This then happened to four other men.

Then the guru came out of the tent with all of the five men, unharmed. The blood on his sword had been goat's blood. These five courageous Sikhs now formed the basis of the especially pure ones who became the founder members of an elite community within the Sikhs.

They were called *Khalsa* (the pure or dedicated ones), and have been likened to soldier-saints.

They carefully followed the Sikh Code of Conduct and conventions. They wore the outward emblems of belonging to the *Khalsa* – the "five Ks" – so that everyone would recognize them as Sikhs.

The five Ks

The five symbols of the Sikh faith all begin with the letter K in Punjabi and so are known as the five Ks.

1. Kesh

This is uncut hair which symbolizes obedience to God and holiness.

2. Kangha

This is a wooden comb symbolizing cleanliness and inner purity.

3. Kachh

These are shorts which are worn underneath other clothes and symbolize goodness, chastity and alertness.

4. Kara

This steel bracelet, which symbolizes eternity, is worn on the right wrist. It also indicates that a Sikh is in bondage to God.

5. Kirpan

This small sword, symbolizing strength and courage, is a sign that the wearer defends the faith and protects the poor.

The turban

The turban, perhaps the most distinctive feature of a *Khalsa*, was not one of the five Ks but was added to them.

Khalsa Sikh men are easy to recognize as they wear full beards and their uncut hair is contained in their turbans.

F.A.Qs

Q: How many Sikhs are there?
A: There are about 16-18 million Sikhs in the world.

Q: How big is Sikhism in comparison with the other largest world religions?
A: Sikhism ranks as the world's fifth largest religion.

Q: Where do Sikhs live today?
A: 80% of Sikhs live in the Punjab.

- About 500,000 live in Britain.
- About 225,000 live in Canada.
- About 100,000 Sikhs live in the USA.

Q: Is the Sikh faith a missionary religion?
A: No. It does not try to win outsiders to its faith but concentrates on the members of its own community and on its own devotion to God.

Q: How does it compare with the other world monotheistic religions?
A: It is the youngest of the four great monotheistic religions.

Q: Is it right to view Sikhism as a variety of Hinduism?
A: No. And to do so greatly offends Sikhs.

"I observe neither Hindu fasting nor the ritual of the Muslim Ramadan month; him I serve who at the last shall save. The Lord of universe of the Hindus, Gosain and Allah to me are one; from Hindus and Muslims have I broken free. I perform neither Kaaba pilgrimage nor at bathing spots worship; one sole Lord I serve, and no other. I perform neither the Hindu worship nor the Muslim prayer; To the sole formless Lord in my heart I bow. We neither are Hindus nor Muslims; Our body and life belong to the one supreme Being who alone is both Ram and Allah for us." *Guru Arjan Dev, Guru Granth Sahib, Raga Bhairon pg. 1136*

6 JUDAISM

TIME-LINE

BCE means "before the common era" (= Christian "BC"). CE means "of the common era" (= Christian "AD").

BCE

c. 2000	Patriarchs in Canaan. Nomadic.
c. 1600	Joseph becomes Prime Minister in Egypt. Jews are later made slaves to the Egyptians.
c. 1250	Exodus from Egypt.
c. 1200 –1020	Israelite conquest of Canaan.
c. 1020 –922	United monarchy.
c. 1020 –1000	Saul: Israel's first king.
c. 1000 –961	David: Israel's second king.
c. 961 –922	Solomon: Israel's third king, builds first Temple in Jerusalem.
c. 922	Divided monarchy.
722	Fall of northern kingdom and exile of 10 northern tribes.
586	Jerusalem Temple destroyed, Babylonian exile begins.
538	Cyrus' edict allows Jews to return to Jerusalem.
c. 515	Completion of the rebuilding of the Second Temple in Jerusalem.
c. 332	Alexander the Great occupies Judea.
167	Seleucid king Antiochus desecrates the Temple, beginning of the Maccabean Revolt.
164	Temple retaken by Maccabees; purification and rededication of Temple.
63	Roman General Pompei invited to support Hyrcanus; Hyrcanus becomes high priest, Antipater becomes administrator of Judea; loss of Jewish independence.
40	Herod (Antipater's son) recognized in Rome as King of Judea (now called Palestine).

6	Rome assumes direct rule in Judea.
26–36	Pontius Pilate procurator (governor) of Palestine.
66–70	Great Revolt, ending in destruction of Herod's Temple.
73	Fall of Masada.
132 –135	Bar-Cochba leads Jewish rebellion against the Romans.
135	Jerusalem destroyed, dispersion of Jews.
200	*Mishnah* codified.
212	Jews become citizens of the Roman Empire: large communities in Spain, France, South Germany, Italy, Greece, and Asia Minor.
500	*Gemara* written down. Babylonian *Talmud* compiled.
800	Charlemagne and the Pope invite Jews to settle in the Holy Roman Empire.
c. 950	First Jews arrive in Poland.
1096	First crusade.
1783	Mendelssohn and the beginning of Berlin *Haskala* (Jewish Enlightenment).
1810 –1874	Abraham Geiger (Reform Movement).
1801 –1875	Zachariah Frankel (Conservative Movement).
1820s	Spread of *Haskala* (Jewish Enlightenment) to Austrian Galicia.
1830s	Beginnings of sizable German-Jewish immigration to the United States.
May 14, 1948	Declaration of the State of Israel and beginning of the War for Independence – Israel invaded by five Arab states.
1967	Six Day War: Jerusalem reunited, under control of Israel.
1972	Ordination of first (Reform) Jewish woman rabbi in US.
May 1998	Israel celebrates its 50th anniversary.

The history of Judaism – the Patriarchs

> How odd
> Of God
> To choose
> The Jews.
> *William Norman Ewer*
>
> But not so odd
> As those who choose
> A Jewish God,
> But spurn the Jews.
> *Cecil Browne, replying to William Ewer*

Abram (Abraham) and the origins of Judaism

The origin and history of the Jews is recorded in the Hebrew scriptures (the Old Testament of the Christian Bible). God called one person and his family to follow him and, against all human probability, promised to make his descendants into God's people.

"The Lord had said to Abram, 'Leave your country, your people and your father's household and go to the land I will show you. I will make you into a great nation and I will bless you." *Genesis 12:1-2.*

In response to God's call Abram and his wife Sarai traveled from Haran in northern Mesopotamia to settle in the hills of southern Canaan.

The Patriarchs

Abraham, his son Isaac and grandson Jacob – the Patriarchs – are the physical and spiritual ancestors of Judaism.

The Patriarchs' God was known as

Elohim (El) and is referred to variously as El Shaddai (God of the mountains or God Almighty), El Elyon (God Most High), and El Olam (God everlasting). The Patriarchs practiced animal sacrifice and circumcision.

Isaac

In Jewish tradition God's command to Abraham to sacrifice Isaac as a burnt offering (Genesis 22) is known as the *Akeidah* (the "Binding," a reference to the fact that Isaac was bound on the altar). According to Jewish teachings, it demonstrated Isaac's great faith, because he knew that he was going to be sacrificed and did not resist.

Isaac later married Rebecca and they had twin boys – Jacob and Esau (Genesis 25).

Jacob (Israel) and the children of Israel

Jacob's 12 sons: Reuben, Simeon, Levi, Judah, Zebulun, Issachar, Dan, Gad, Asher, Naphtali, Joseph and Benjamin – are the ancestors of the "tribes" (or clans). There is no tribe of Joseph but two tribes were descended from his two sons Manasseh and Ephraim.

Joseph

After being sold as a slave in Egypt, Joseph rose to be Pharaoh's vizier (the highest executive office in Egypt). Subsequently, as a result of a famine in Canaan, Joseph's family traveled to Egypt where, at Pharaoh's invitation, they settled in Goshen in the Nile delta.

THE TEN COMMANDMENTS

And God spake all these words, saying,

1. I am the LORD thy God, which have brought thee out of the land of Egypt, out of the house of bondage. Thou shalt have no other gods before me.

2. Thou shalt not make unto thee any graven image, or any likeness of any thing that is in heaven above, or that is in the earth beneath, or that is in the water under the earth: Thou shalt not bow down thyself to them, nor serve them: for I the LORD thy God am a jealous God, visiting the iniquity of the fathers upon the children unto the third and fourth generation of them that hate me; And showing mercy unto thousands of them that love me, and keep my commandments.

3. Thou shalt not take the name of the LORD thy God in vain; for the LORD will not hold him guiltless that taketh his name in vain.

4. Remember the sabbath day, to keep it holy. Six days shalt thou labor, and do all thy work: But the seventh day is the sabbath of the LORD thy God: in it thou shalt not do any work, thou, nor thy son, nor thy daughter, thy manservant, nor thy maidservant, nor thy cattle, nor thy stranger that is within thy gates: For in six days the LORD made heaven and earth, the sea, and all that in them is, and rested the seventh day: wherefore the LORD blessed the sabbath day, and hallowed it.

5. Honor thy father and thy mother: that thy days may be long upon the land which the LORD thy God giveth thee.

6. Thou shalt not kill.

7. Thou shalt not commit adultery.

8. Thou shalt not steal.

9. Thou shalt not bear false witness against thy neighbor.

10. Thou shalt not covet thy neighbor's house, thou shalt not covet thy neighbor's wife, nor his manservant, nor his maidservant, nor his ox, nor his ass, nor any thing that is thy neighbor's.
Exodus 20:1-17, KJV

The Exodus and the giving of the *Torah*

Some 200 years after Joseph died, the Egyptians were alarmed to find that they had become a sizable foreign population – the descendants of Joseph and his brothers. Pharaoh forced these people to work in labor gangs on his building sites and treated them savagely. God then intervened to rescue the slaves from Egypt. This miraculous deliverance under the leadership of Moses, the giving of the Ten Commandments, their forty years wandering in the wilderness and conquest of the "promised land" still govern the religious consciousness, holidays and observances of Jews today.

The history of Judaism – from the Judges to the Diaspora

Judges and kings

After their occupation of Canaan the Israelites were ruled by different judges before Samuel anointed their first king – King Saul. Saul was succeeded by Israel's greatest king – King David. After the death of David's son, King Solomon, the nation was split into two kingdoms: the kingdom of Judah and the kingdom of Israel (1 Kings 12; 2 Chronicles 10).

The northern kingdom, Israel, was destroyed by the Assyrians in 721 BCE and the ten tribes which made up this nation disappeared. The southern kingdom, Judah, survived the Assyrian years but was conquered by the Babylonians in 586 BCE when the temple was destroyed and the people were led off into exile.

The exile

It was during the exile, when the Jews were without their temple, that Judaism had its origins. This period saw the rise of synagogues (the word means "coming together" or "meeting place") and a life centered on the *Torah* – the law of Moses. The scribes became interpreters of the law. It was while the people were in exile in Babylonia that they began to be called Jews.

After the exile

When the Persians permitted the Jews to return from exile (538 BCE), Jerusalem and its temple were rebuilt.

Alexander the Great conquered the Persian Empire in 331 BCE and the small province of Judea came under Greek control in 332. Upon Alexander's death Judea was ruled first by the Ptolemies and then by the Seleucids. The Jews rebelled against the Seleucid ruler, Antiochus IV Epiphanes, and in 142 BCE gained their independence. They remained self-governing until the Romans came in 63 BCE. It was the Romans who gave this small parcel of land the name Palestine.

In CE 66 Zealots were prepared to fight for national independence. They rebelled against Roman rule with the result that in CE 70 the Roman armies under Titus, destroyed the Temple. The

THE NAME "JEW"
HEBREWS
The people now called Jews were originally known as Hebrews. The word "Hebrew" is first used in the *Torah* to describe Abraham: "One who had escaped came and reported this to Abram the Hebrew" (Genesis 14:13).
ISRAELITES
The name Children of Israel or Israelites refers to the fact that the people are descendants of Jacob, who was given the name "Israel" ("the one who wrestled with God" or "the Champion of God") after wrestling all night with an angel.
JEW
The word "Jew" (in Hebrew *Yehudi*) is derived from the name Judah, the name of the southern kingdom, which, with its capital Jerusalem, was captured by the Babylonians.

Jews were totally defeated and scattered in the "Diaspora" (dispersion).

The destruction of the Temple

Judaism came into full existence after the destruction of the Temple in CE 70.

The religious life of the Jews now centered around the *Torah* (Law) and the synagogue.

The Diaspora

Babylon then became the center of Jewish learning. It was here the *Gemara* (a commentary on the *Mishnah*) was compiled. The *Gemara* and the *Mishnah* together are known as the *Talmud*.

From CE 847 the Jewish community in Babylon waned under persecution by Muslim rulers; and Spanish Jews became the leaders of worldwide Judaism. Their greatest leader was the philosopher Maimonides (1138–1204). In 1391 there was a massacre of thousands of Jews in Spain; in 1492 the Jews and the Moors were expelled from that country.

By this time the Jews had spread to many Mediterranean countries. After the Jews had been persecuted by the Christians in the crusades, many fled to Poland. By the end of the sixteenth century Poland had the largest concentration of Jews in the world. Their language was Yiddish – a combination of German and Hebrew. In the seventeenth century Jews in European cities were herded into ghettos (legally enforced restricted areas for residence). These were always in the worst parts of the cities.

Moses Mendelssohn (1729–1786), a learned Jewish philosopher who lived in Berlin, campaigned for the emancipation of the Jews, encouraging them to come out of the ghettos and enter the modern world. At the same time Baal Shem Tov (1699–1760) began preaching that God was not found in the academic formalism and teachings on the Jewish scriptures and the *Talmud*. But God was found in simple heartfelt faith. His followers became known as the Hasidim (pious ones) and to this day they continue to oppose secularism in modern Jewish life.

The history of Judaism – the land of Israel

The Promised Land

God promised Abraham and his descendants a new home in the land of Canaan (Genesis 12:2). This land is often referred to as the Promised Land because of God's repeated promise to give the land to the descendants of Abraham (Genesis 12:7; 13:15; 15:18; 17:8).

Jews have lived in this land continuously from the time of its original conquest by Joshua (more than 3,200 years ago) until the present day, even though they have not always been in political control of the land. The land of Israel is central to Judaism. Some rabbis have declared that it is a *mitzvah* (commandment, found in Numbers 33:53) to take possession of Israel and to live in it.

Many Jews think of living outside of Israel as an unnatural state. The world outside Israel is often referred to as *galut*, which is usually translated as "diaspora" (dispersion). A more literal translation would be "exile" or "captivity." When

Jews live outside Israel, they are living in exile from their land.

Jews were exiled from the land of Israel by the Romans in CE 135, and did not have any control over the land again until CE 1948.

Zionism and the state of Israel

When they were dispersed by the Romans, the Jewish people never gave up hope that they would one day return to their home in Israel. That hope was expressed in the song *Ha-Tikvah* (The Hope) – the anthem of the Zionist movement and the state of Israel.

Ha-Tikvah (The Hope)

As long as deep within the heart
The Jewish soul is warm
And toward the edges of the east
An eye to Zion looks
Our hope is not yet lost,
The hope of two thousand years
To be a free people in our own land
In the land of Zion and Jerusalem.
To be a free people in our own land
In the land of Zion and Jerusalem.

Herzl and Weizmann

For a long time, this desire for their homeland was merely a vague hope. However, in the late 1800s, at a time when the Jewish population was being decimated in Russia, Theodor Herzl and Chaim Weizmann realized that Jewish people would never be treated fairly until they had a land of their own. They

founded a political movement dedicated to the creation of a Jewish state in Israel. This movement became known as Zionism. The name "Zionism" comes from the word "Zion," the name of a stronghold in Jerusalem. It later applied to Jerusalem in general and then to the Jewish idea of utopia.

Early Zionists were so desperate for a refuge that at one point they actually considered a proposal to create a Jewish homeland in Uganda.

The Balfour Declaration

After World War One the land of Israel was part of Palestine, a British protectorate which included Israel and parts of Jordan and Egypt. In a letter from British foreign secretary Lord Balfour to Jewish financier Lord Rothschild the British government expressed a commitment to creating a Jewish homeland in Palestine. This letter is commonly known as the Balfour Declaration of 1917. After the declaration Jewish immigration to Israel expanded rapidly, but little progress was made toward the establishment of a Jewish state until after the Holocaust destroyed a third of the world's Jewish population.

May 14, 1948

The newly founded United Nations developed a partition plan dividing Palestine into Jewish and Arab portions. The new State of Israel was proclaimed on May 14, 1948.

Persecution of Jews

PERSECUTION OF JEWS THROUGH THE CENTURIES	
1096	Massacre of Rhineland Jews by crusaders.
1190	Massacre of Jews at York, England.
1290	Expulsion of Jews from England.
1394	(Second) Expulsion of Jews from France.
1492	Expulsion of Jews from Spain.
1555	Jews of Rome ordered into a ghetto.
1648	Chmielnitsky massacres in Eastern Europe.
1825-1855	Severe oppression under Nicholas I Czar of Russia.
1881-1882	Wave of pogroms in Russia leads to mass East European Jewish immigration to the United States.
1933-1945	The Shoah (Holocaust) when 6 million Jews were killed.

Opposition to and persecution of the Jews has not been confined to the horrors of World War II. Throughout the centuries Jews have suffered under many unjust laws in scores of countries. In England Jews were not allowed to be members of Parliament until 1858; and no Jews could take degrees at Oxford and Cambridge universities until 1871.

Extermination by gas under the Nazis

From January 1940 in Germany Jews were killed as part of the so-called "Euthanasia," – the extermination of "lives not worthy to live", the handicapped, mentally ill and terminally ill.

About 120,000 Jews were killed under the Nazi "euthanasia" project. In total six million Jews were killed under the Nazis.

Auschwitz commandant at his trial at Nuremberg, 1945

"I was ordered to establish extermination facilities at Auschwitz in June 1941. I visited Treblinka to find out how they carried out their exterminations. The camp commandant told me that he had liquidated 80,000 people in six months. He used carbon monoxide gas and I didn't think his methods were very efficient. So, at Auschwitz, I used Cyclon B. It took from 3 to 15 minutes to kill the people in the chamber. We knew when the people were dead because their screaming stopped. After their bodies were removed, our special commandos took off the rings and extracted the gold from the teeth of the corpses. Another improvement we made over Treblinka was that we built our gas chambers to take 2,000 people at one time." *Auschwitz commandant*

Hitler

"My feelings as a Christian point me to my Lord and Savior as a fighter. It points me to the man who once in loneliness, surrounded by a few followers, recognized these Jews for what they were and summoned men to

EXTERMINATION CAMPS

KULMHOF (CHELMNO)

1941, 1942, 1944

Carbon monoxide from car exhaust killed more than 150,000 Jews.

BELZEC

1942

6 large gas chambers killed 600,000 Jews.

SOBIBOR

1942, 1943

6 gas chambers killed at least 200,000 Jews.

TREBLINKA

1942, 1943

13 gas chambers killed 700,000 Jews.

MAJDANEK

1942, 1943

Mass shootings killed 24,000 Jews.

1942, 1943, 1944

Three carbon monoxide gas chambers, and one chamber using Zyklon B (a highly poisonous insecticide made from cyan hydrogen) killed 50,000.

AUSCHWITZ-BIRKENAU

1942, 1943, 1944

9 gas chambers killed more than one million Jews.

MAUTHAUSEN (UPPER AUSTRIA)

1941

1 gas chamber, using Zyklon B, killed at least 4,000 Jews.

NEUENGAMME (SOUTH-EAST OF HAMBURG)

1942

1 gas chamber, using Zyklon B, killed at least 450 Jews.

SACHSENHAUSEN

1943

1 gas chamber, using Zyklon B, killed several thousand Jews.

STUTTHOF

1944

1 gas chamber, using Zyklon B, killed over 1,000 Jews.

RAVENSBRUECK

1945

1 gas chamber killed more than 2,300 Jews.

fight against them and who, God's truth! was greatest not as a sufferer but as a fighter. In boundless love as a Christian and as a man I read through the passage which tells us how the Lord at last rose in his might and seized the scourge to drive out of the Temple the brood of vipers and adders. How terrific was his fight against the Jewish poison. Today, after two thousand years, with deepest emotion I recognize more profoundly than ever before the fact that it was for this that he had to shed his blood upon the cross. As a Christian I have no duty to allow myself to be cheated, but I have the duty to be a fighter for truth and justice…And if there is anything which could demonstrate that we are acting rightly, it is the distress that daily grows. For as a Christian I have also a duty to my own people. And when I look on my people I see them work and work and toil and labor, and at the end of the week they have only for their wages wretchedness and misery. When I go out in the morning and see these men standing in their queues and look into their pinched faces, then I believe I would be no Christian, but a very devil, if I felt no pity for them, if I did not, as did our Lord two thousand years ago, turn against those by whom today this poor people are plundered and exposed." *Adolf Hitler*

The writings of Judaism

The most important prayers recited in synagogues are the *Shema* (Hear) and the Prayer of the 18 Benedictions.

The *Shema*

"Hear, O Israel: The LORD our God is one LORD: And thou shalt love the LORD thy God with all thine heart, and with all thy soul, and with all thy might. And these words, which I command thee this day, shall be in thine heart: And thou shalt teach them diligently unto thy children, and shalt talk of them when thou sittest in thine house, and when thou walkest by the way, and when thou liest down, and when thou risest up. And thou shalt bind them for a sign upon thine hand, and they shall be as frontlets between thine eyes. And thou shalt write them upon the posts of thy house, and on thy gates." *Deuteronomy 6:4-9 KJV*

Where Jewish beliefs are found
The *Tanakh*

The Jewish Bible (the Christian's Old Testament) is called the *Tanakh*. This word is derived from the Hebrew letters of the three parts that make it up: *Torah*, *Nevi'im*, and *Ketuvim*. For Jews, the *Tanakh* is the Written Law.

The *Torah*

Jewish religious life is guided by the commandments and principles contained in the *Torah*. The word "Torah" can mean:

- A scroll made from kosher animal parchment with the entire text of the Five Books of Moses written in it by a *sofer* (a ritual scribe).
- The five Books of Moses written in any format (also called the *Chumash*, the Pentateuch and the Five Books of Moses).
- The *Tanakh*.
- The entire corpus of Jewish law. This

includes the Written and the Oral Law. It which includes the *Talmud* and the *Midrash*.

The Jewish scriptures
1. *Torah*
Books of Genesis, Exodus, Leviticus, Numbers and Deuteronomy.

2. Prophets
Books of Joshua, Judges, 1 Samuel, 2 Samuel, 1 Kings, 2 Kings, Isaiah, Jeremiah, Ezekiel, Hosea, Joel, Amos, Obadiah, Jonah, Micah, Nahum, Habukkuk, Zephaniah, Haggai, Zechariah and Malachi. (The last 12 are sometimes grouped together as "*Trei Asar*." ["Twelve"])

3. Writings
Books of Psalms, Proverbs, Job, Song of Songs, Ruth, Lamentations, Ecclesiastes, Esther, Daniel, Ezra and Nehemiah, 1 Chronicles and 2 Chronicles.

The Oral Law
The *Torah* requires more information than is given in the text alone. Many terms and definitions used in the Written Law are undefined while concepts such as *shekhita* (slaughtering of animals in a kosher fashion), divorce and the rights of the firstborn are not elaborated.

This indicates that it was transmitted side by side with an oral tradition. The *Mishnah* is a compilation of the Oral Law and was written down around CE 200.

The *Talmud*
The word "talmud" literally means "study." The *Talmud* is the supreme source book of Law taking the principles presented in the *Torah* and applying them to different circumstances.

The word "Talmud" generally applies to the Babylonian *Talmud*.

It contains stories, laws, medical knowledge, and debates about moral choices. The material comes from two main sources:

- The *Mishnah*
- The *Gemera* (one Babylonian and one Palestinian) which is an assembly of comments on the Mishnah from hundreds of rabbis from CE 200–500.

The *Midrash*
The term "Midrash" is based on a Hebrew word meaning "interpretation" or "exegesis" and refers to a particular way of reading and interpreting a biblical verse. Thus we may say that the ancient rabbis provided *Midrash* to Scripture.

"*Midrash* is a method of reading the Bible as an eternal text, and is the result of applying a set of hermeneutical principles evolved by the community to guide one in reading the canon, in order to focus one's reading. The ultimate goal of *midrash* is to 'search out' the fullness of what was spoken by the Divine Voice." *Dr Charles T. Davis.*

Key Jewish beliefs

Jewish beliefs

- God is the creator and absolute ruler of the universe.
- Judaism affirms the inherent goodness of the world and its people as creations of God. Believers are able to sanctify their lives and draw closer to God by fulfilling *mitzvot* (divine commandments). No savior is needed as an intermediary.
- The Jews are God's chosen people.
- The Ten Commandments form the core of Jewish life.
- The need to follow the many dietary and other laws of the *Torah*.

God's nature
God exists

The *Torah* does not set about trying to prove God's existence but simply states it: "In the beginning, God created..." If proof for the existence for God were needed, then the existence of the universe would be sufficient.

God is One

The *Shema* is the primary expression of the Jewish faith. It begins, "Hear, Israel: The Lord is our God, the Lord is one."

These opening words can be translated as, "The Lord is our God, the Lord alone," meaning that Jews should not pray to any other god. Jews recite the *Shema* every morning and evening.

God created everything

Everything in the universe was created by God and only by God. "I am the Lord, and there is none else. I form the light and create darkness: I make peace and create evil: I the Lord do these things." *Isaiah 45:6-7, KJV*

God is incorporeal

Judaism maintains that God has no body. When parts of God's body (his hands, his wings) are mentioned in Scripture and the *Talmud*, these are used anthropomorphically.

Jews are forbidden to represent God in a physical form as this is thought to be idolatrous.

The *moshiach* (or the Messiah)

"I believe with perfect faith in the coming of the *moshiach*, and though he may tarry, still I await him every day." (Principle 12 of the 13 Principles of the Faith)

The *Shemoneh Esrei* prayer, which Jews pray three times a day, includes prayers for:

- the coming of the *moshiach*;
- the coming together of the exiles;
- the restoration of the religious courts of justice;
- an end of wickedness, sin and heresy, and reward for the righteous;
- the rebuilding of Jerusalem;
- the restoration of the line of King David;
- the restoration of Temple service.

The word *moshiach* literally means "the anointed one." It refers back to the days when kings were anointed with oil when they took the throne.

The word does not mean "savior" and should not be confused with the Christian concept of Savior. The *moshiach* will be a great political and military leader descended from King David (Jeremiah 23:5) who will win battles for Israel. He will be a great judge making righteous decisions (Jeremiah 33:15). But above all he will be a human being, not a god, demi-god or other supernatural being.

Resurrection

Belief in the eventual resurrection of the dead is a fundamental belief of traditional Judaism. Jews believe that when the Messiah comes to initiate the perfect world of peace and prosperity, the righteous dead will be brought back to life and given the opportunity to experience the perfected world that their righteousness helped to create. The wicked dead will not be resurrected.

Sages and scholars
Hillel and Shammai
(1st century BCE – CE 1st century)

These two great scholars were contemporaries and the leaders of two opposing schools of thought (known as "houses").

The *Talmud* records over 300 differences of opinion between Beit Hillel (the House of Hillel) and Beit Shammai (the House of Shammai). In almost every one of these disputes, Hillel's view prevailed.

Rabbi Yochanan ben Zakkai

Rabbi Yochanan ben Zakkai, the most distinguished disciple of Rabbi Hillel, has been called the "father of wisdom and the father of generations (of scholars)" because he ensured the continuation of Jewish scholarship after Jerusalem fell to Rome in CE 70.

According to tradition, ben Zakkai was a pacifist in Jerusalem in CE 68 when the city was under siege by General Vespasian. Jerusalem, however, was controlled by the Zealots who would rather die than surrender to Rome.

The Zealots would not listen to Ben Zakkai's talk of surrender, so ben Zakkai faked his own death and had his disciples smuggle him out of Jerusalem in a coffin. They carried the coffin to Vespasian's tent where ben Zakkai then emerged from the coffin and told Vespasian about a vision he had seen in which Vespasian became emperor.

Ben Zakkai asked Vespasian to set aside a place in Yavneh (near modern Rehovot) where he could move his *yeshivah* (school) and study the *Torah* in peace. Vespasian promised that if the prophesy came true he would grant ben Zakkai's request. Vespasian became emperor and kept his word, allowing the school to be established after the war was over. The *yeshiva* survived and became the focus of Jewish learning for centuries.

This academy became the site of the Sanhedrin, and assured the continuation of Judaism.

Commandments, articles of faith and theological schools

613 Commandments

Judaism teaches that in the *Torah* God gave the Jews 613 commandments. Jews have to carefully observe all these commandments, but they are not binding on non-Jews.

Here are eight examples of the 613 commandments:

God

To love God (Deuteronomy 6:5).

Torah

To learn the *Torah* and to teach it (Deuteronomy 6:7).

Signs and symbols

To circumcise the male offspring (Genesis 17:12; Leviticus 12:3).

To put *tzitzit* (tassels) on the corners of clothing (Numbers 15:38).

To love others

Not to stand by idly when a human life is in danger (Leviticus 19:16).

The poor

To leave the gleanings for the poor (Leviticus 19:9).

To give charity according to one's means (Deuteronomy 15:11).

Treatment of Gentiles

To love the stranger (Deuteronomy 10:19).

Marriage

To be fruitful and multiply (Genesis 1:28).

Festivals

To celebrate the festivals (Passover, Pentecost and Tabernacles) (Exodus 23:14).

13 Articles of Faith

Rabbi Moshe ben Maimon (1135-1204), known as Maimonides in English, formulated the influential *13 Principles of the Faith*.

Jews base their beliefs on the Old Testament even though Judaism has no formal set of beliefs that one must hold to be a Jew. Most Jews, however, accept the *13 Principles of the Faith*.

13 Principles of the Faith

- God exists.
- God is one and unique.
- God is incorporeal (is without any material form).
- God is eternal. God has always existed and was never created.
- Prayer and worship is to be directed to God alone.
- The words of the prophets are true.
- Moses was the greatest of the prophets.
- The Written *Torah* and Oral *Torah* were given to Moses at Mount Sinai.
- There will be no other *Torah*.
- God is omniscient (knows the thoughts and deeds of men).
- God will reward the good and punish the wicked in the after-life.
- The Messiah will come.
- The dead will be resurrected.

Theological schools

There are four divisions or theological schools within modern Judaism: Orthodox, Conservative, Reform and Reconstructionist.

These schools are divided in their approach to the Jewish scriptures:

The *Orthodox* say that the scriptures are absolute because they are the unchanging laws from God.

The *Conservative* agree that they are the laws from God but believe that they change and evolve.

The *Reform* and *Reconstructionist* say that they are simply guidelines and one is under no obligation to follow them.

Orthodox

This is the oldest and most conservative form of Judaism. Orthodox Jews attempt to remain as close as possible to the original form of their religion. They are rigorous about ritual observances, the dietary laws and keeping the Sabbath. They stress the absolute authority of revealed Law and regard every word in their sacred texts as being divinely inspired. They do not accept that it can evolve. There are no Orthodox women rabbis.

Conservative

Conservative Judaism is a main-line movement midway between Reform and Orthodox.

It began in the mid-nineteenth century as a reaction against the Reform movement. While they obey the *Torah*

they claim the right to adapt the interpretation of the traditions as they apply to the modern world. As a result men and women sit together in the synagogue, women become rabbis and long distance journeys to attend Sabbath services are allowed. Even so, food must be kosher.

Reform

Reformed Judaism stresses the ethical teachings of the prophets and the growth of an age of justice, truth and peace.

Reformed Jews are a liberal group who allow individuals to decide whether to follow or ignore the dietary laws or other traditional laws. They have adopted modern forms of worship.

Reconstructionist

Reconstructionist Judaism is a new and small liberal movement started by Mordecai Kaplan (1881–1983) as an attempt to unify and revitalize Judaism. In 1935 the bi-weekly *Reconstructionist* periodical appeared with the following statement of belief: "Dedicated to the advancement of Judaism as a religious civilization, to the up-building of the land of Israel as the spiritual center of the Jewish people, and to the furtherance of universal freedom, justice and peace."

Reconstructionist Jews do not believe that the Jewish law is binding. They also reject the idea that the Jews are the chosen people.

Jewish practices

Sabbath observance

- Observance of the Sabbath (day of rest) starting at sundown on Friday evening.
- Strict religious discipline governs almost all areas of life.
- Regular attendance at synagogue.
- Celebration of the annual festivals.

The Chief Rabbis in France and Great Britain have authority only by the agreement of those who accept it. Two Chief Rabbis in Israel have civil authority in areas of family law.

Shabbat

Celebrated every Saturday both at home and in the synagogue, from sundown Friday to sundown Saturday, the Sabbath (*Shabbat*) is the most important ritual observance in Judaism and the only ritual observance instituted in the Ten Commandments. It is primarily a day of rest and spiritual enrichment. The word "Shabbat" comes from the Hebrew word *Shin-Bet-Tav* meaning to cease, to end, or to rest. Jews have long revered the Sabbath as a "taste of the world to come."

Shabbat involves two interrelated commandments: to remember (*zachor*) *Shabbat*, and to observe (*shamor*) *Shabbat*.

Zachor

Jews are commanded to remember *Shabbat*, that is, to remember the significance of Shabbat as a commemoration of creation and as a commemoration of deliverance from slavery in Egypt (Exodus 20:11; Deuteronomy 5:15). Jews remember these two meanings of *Shabbat* when they recite *kiddush* (the prayer over wine sanctifying *Shabbat*).

Shamor

Traditionally, rabbis have taught that the work prohibited on *Shabbat* is the type of work that went into building the sanctuary. They found 39 categories of forbidden tasks including: work, cooking, traveling, buying and selling, gathering wood and kindling a fire. Today, the use of electricity is prohibited because it serves the same function as fire.

As with almost all of the commandments, all of these *Shabbat* restrictions can be violated to save a life.

Circumcision

Ritual circumcision is a sign of God's everlasting covenant with the Jewish people (Genesis 17). Later, God told Moses, "On the eighth day the boy is to be circumcised" (Leviticus 12:3). During circumcision the fold of skin (foreskin) at the end of the penis is cut off. This serves as a constant reminder that he is a descendant of Abraham and a servant of the almighty God.

The *mohel*

The *mohel* who performs the ritual circumcision is a person who has received specialized training in the medical and ritual aspects of the *bris* (the rite of circumcision). He is a master surgeon in his particular area of expertise. A Rabbi, cantor or spiritual leader may serve his community as a *mohel*. The process itself takes less than 30 seconds during which the *mohel*: first, recites a Hebrew blessing; amputates the foreskin with a sterilized scalpel; quickly splits the mucous with (disinfected) thumbnails; applies suction; and completes the procedure by bandaging the wound.

Bar Mitzvah

Boys reach the status of Bar Mitzvah on their thirteenth birthday. Bar Mitzvah literally means the "son of the commandment." "*Bar*" is "son" in Aramaic. "*Mitzvah*" is "commandment" in both Hebrew and Aramaic.

The Bar Mitzvah ceremony formally recognizes the boys as adults. They are now personally responsible for keeping the Jewish commandments and laws.

The boys are allowed to lead a religious service, can sign contracts, testify in religious courts, and, theoretically, can marry (though the *Talmud* recommends 18 to 24 as the proper age for marriage).

Today's popular Bar Mitzvah ceremony is not required, and does not fulfil any commandment. It is a relatively modern innovation, not mentioned in the *Talmud*, and the elaborate ceremonies and receptions that are commonplace today were unheard of as recently as a century ago.

Jewish fasts, feasts and festivals

The Jewish calender

The Jewish calendar is not based on the earth's rotation around the sun (as the secular calendar is) but on the cycles of the moon so that each new moon marks the start of a new month. Jewish holidays therefore fall on different dates each year according to the secular calendar, but on the same date according to the Jewish calendar.

New Year Festival (*Rosh Hashanah*)

A ram's horn blown in the synagogue announces the beginning of the New Year Festival – often called the "Feast of the Trumpets." The official Jewish New Year's Day (*Rosh Hashanah*, "Head of the Year") begins a ten-day festival when Jews spend ten days looking back over the past year and asking for forgiveness. They eat "sweet foods" and apples dipped in honey as a symbol of the good year to come. Jews believe that during this ten-day period God judges each person's deeds, deciding who shall live and who shall die in the year to come.

Day of Atonement (*Yom Kippur*)

Yom Kippur, the last day of the *Rosh-Hashanah,* is the most solemn day of the year. Before the destruction of the Temple it was the only day on which the High Priest could go into the Holy of Holies to ask forgiveness for the previous year and God's blessing for the coming year.

Many Jews who do not observe any other Jewish custom will refrain from work, fast and attend synagogue services on this day. It is a day set aside to "afflict the soul" to atone for the sins of the past year. Jews spend most of this day in the

MAIN JEWISH FEASTS, FASTS AND FESTIVALS			
English name	Jewish name	Secular calendar	Jewish calendar
New Year Festival	Rosh Hashanah	September or October	Tishri 1
Day of Atonement	Yom Kippur	September or October	Tishri 10
Festival of Tabernacles	Sukkot	September or October	Tishri 15-22
Feast of Dedication	Hanukkah	November or December	Kislev 25-30
Feast of Lots	Purim	February or March	Adar 14
Festival of Passover	Pesach	March or April	Nisan 14
Feast of Unleavened Bread	Massot	March or April	Nisan 15-21
Feast of Pentecost	Shavuot	May or June	Sivan 6
Fast of the fifth month	Tishah B'Av	July or August	Av 5

synagogue praying for forgiveness and
they fast for the whole day. *Yom Kippur* is
a complete Sabbath and no work can be
performed. One long blast on the *shofar*
concludes the day and Jews have now
entered into the new year.

Festival of Tabernacles (*Sukkot*, also called Festival of Booths, Festival of Ingathering)

Starting five days after *Yom Kippur* this
week-long festival, commemorates the
40 years that the Israelites spent
wandering through the desert after their
exodus from Egypt. It is also one of the
three harvest festivals and is a joyful
time.

On *Sukkot* traditional Jews construct
small open-roofed booth-like buildings
in which they may camp out to recall
God's provision for his people in the
desert.

Feast of Dedication (*Hanukkah*, also called the Festival of Lights)

This festival commemorates the
purification and rededication of the
Temple by Judas Maccabaeus in 164
BCE and his victory over the Syrian
army of Antiochus Epiphanes (165

BCE). It is an eight-day celebration of
religious freedom. During this festival,
many families light an eight-branched
candlestick – lighting one candle for
each day.

Feast of Purim (Feast of Lots)

The Festival of Purim celebrates the
deliverance from persecution of Jews in
Persia. The event is described in the
book of Esther which tells of Haman's
evil plot and the deliverance of the Jews
after the intervention of Queen Esther
and Mordecai. On the Feast of Purim the
whole book of Esther is read aloud and
whenever Haman's name is mentioned
the congregation boo and stamp their
feet. They send gifts of food to each
other and give to the poor.

Festival of Passover (*Pesach*)

The Festival of Passover celebrates the
exodus when Moses led the Jews out of
slavery in Egypt and into freedom. The
name derives from the night of their
escape when Moses instructed the people
of Israel to smear the doors and lintels of
their homes with blood. At this time the
angel of destruction "passed over" the
firstborn of Israel, but killed the firstborn
of the Egyptians (Exodus 12).

Passover is one of the three Pilgrim
feasts or harvest festivals when Jews
were obliged to attend the Temple at
Jerusalem. (The other two festivals are
Tabernacles and Pentecost.)

But even in Temple times, the primary
focus of Passover was in Jewish homes

and this emphasis has continued. There a ritual *Seder* meal is eaten. In every Jewish home the beginning of Passover starts with this meal and the youngest person present asks, "Why is this night different from all other nights?" The answer is then read from the *Haggadah*, "The Telling," a short book recounting the whole story of the exodus from Egypt.

Feast of the Unleavened Bread (*Massot*)

For seven days after the Passover the Feast of Unleavened Bread is celebrated. During this time Jews eat no normal bread but only the flat, unleavened, cracker-like bread called *matzah*. This is in memory of the first Passover when, according to Jewish tradition, the Jews made their hasty preparations to leave Egypt. They had no time to prepare bread for their journey but instead placed the dough, which had no time to rise and be baked, on their backs, where the sun baked it into *matzah*.

Festival of Pentecost (*Shavuot*, also called the Festival of the First-Fruits, and the Feast of Weeks)

This festival begins in the fiftieth day after the second day of Passover. It is a festival celebrating the wheat harvest and is often called the Festival of First-Fruits because families would bring the first-fruits of the wheat harvest to the Temple. Today, synagogues are decorated with wild flowers and plants. Dairy foods are eaten.

This holiday also commemorates the day God gave the Ten Commandments to Moses at Mount Sinai (Leviticus 23).

Fast of the fifth month (Tishah B'Av)

Jews observe *Tishah B'Av* on the ninth day of the month of Av. According to legend, this was the day on which the Assyrians destroyed the first Temple. It is also the date on which the Second Temple fell to the Romans. Today, ornaments are removed from the synagogues and the day is observed as a day of fasting and mourning.

F.A.Qs (Frequently Asked Questions) about the Jews

Q: Who is a Jew?
A: Judaism may be simply defined as the religion of the Jewish people. But ask the question: "Who is a Jew?" and there are two answers:

- a Jew is any person whose mother was a Jew;
- a Jew is any person who has gone through the formal process of conversion to Judaism.

Being a Jew need not have anything to do with what you believe or what you do nor does living in Israel make you a Jew.

A person born to non-Jewish parents who has not undergone the formal process of conversion but who believes everything that Orthodox Jews believe and observes every law and custom of Judaism is still a non-Jew.

But a person born to a Jewish mother who is an atheist and never practices the Jewish religion is still a Jew.

Once a person has converted to Judaism he is as much a Jew as anyone born Jewish.

Q: Where do the Jews live today?
A: Most Jews live in either the USA (which has over five million Jews) or in Israel (which has over four million Jews).

The only other countries with over a million Jews are Russia and the republics of the former Soviet Union. The six other countries with significant numbers of Jews are Argentina, Brazil, Canada, France, South Africa and the United Kingdom.

The estimated number of Jews in CE 2,000 was about 16 million.

Q: Which three US states have the highest proportion of Jews in their population?
A: 1. New York
   2. New Jersey
   3. Florida.

Q: Who are the religious leaders in Judaism?
A: **Rabbis.**
A rabbi is not a priest. The Hebrew scriptures teach that a priest (*kohein*) is a descendant of Aaron who was charged with performing various rites in the Temple in connection with religious rituals and sacrifices. When the Temple was destroyed priests were no longer needed.

A rabbi is simply a teacher; a person sufficiently educated in *halakhah* (Jewish law) and tradition to instruct the community, and to answer their questions and resolve disputes regarding *halakhah*.

When the Temple was destroyed, rabbis took over the spiritual leadership of the Jewish community. They have a similar role to Christian Protestant ministers, ministering to the community, leading religious services and dealing with many of the administrative matters related to the synagogue.

The local synagogue is governed by the congregation and led by a rabbi who has been chosen by the congregation.

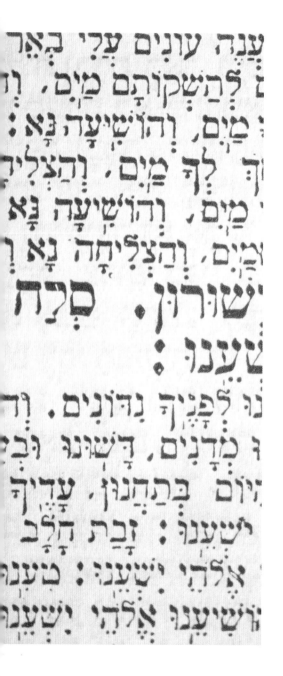

The *chazzan* (cantor)

A *chazzan* (cantor) is the person who leads the congregation in prayer. Any person with a good moral character and a thorough knowledge of the prayers and melodies can lead the prayer services. In many synagogues members of the community lead some or all parts of the prayer service.

One of the most important duties of the *chazzan* is teaching young people to lead all or part of a *Shabbat* service and to chant the *Torah*.

Q: Where do Jews worship?

A: Synagogues.

While it is true that the synagogue is the Jewish equivalent of a church, many important Jewish religious ceremonies are held in the home and not in the synagogue.

Synagogues are the center of the Jewish religious community. They are places for prayer, study and education, as well as for social and charitable work.

A house of prayer

A synagogue is a house of prayer and Jews go to synagogues for community prayer services. While Jews can satisfy the obligations of daily prayer by praying anywhere, there are certain prayers that can only be said in the presence of a *minyan* (a quorum of 10 adult men).

In rabbinical literature the synagogue is sometimes referred to as the "little Temple."

A house of study

A synagogue is usually also a house of study, a *beit midrash*. For the practicing Jew, the study of the sacred texts of Judaism is a life-long task. Most synagogues have well-stocked libraries of sacred Jewish texts for members of the community to study.

Children receive their basic religious education in synagogues.

Synagogue rituals

The sanctuary

Prayer services take place in the sanctuary. Synagogues in the United States are generally designed so that the front of the sanctuary is on the side facing towards Jerusalem. This is the direction that Jews are supposed to face when reciting certain prayers.

The Ark

The most important feature of the sanctuary is the Ark. The name "Ark" is an acrostic of the Hebrew words *Aron Kodesh*. It means "holy cabinet." The Ark is a cabinet housing the *Torah* scrolls.

In front of and slightly above the Ark, is the *ner tamid*, the Eternal Lamp. This lamp symbolizes the commandment to keep a light burning in the tabernacle outside of the curtain surrounding the Ark of the Covenant (Exodus 27:20-21).

The *menorah*

Most synagogues also have a *menorah* (candelabrum) in memory of the *menorah* in the Temple but usually with

six or eight branches instead of the seven branches of the Temple *menorah*. The *menorah* is a symbol of the nation of Israel and its mission to be "a light unto the nations" (Isaiah 42:6).

Q: What do the Jewish symbols mean?
A: *Mezuzah.*

A *mezuzuh* is a small oblong-shaped container fixed to the doorpost of a Jewish house. In the *mezuzah* there is a tiny scroll of parchment with the words of the *Shema* and a companion passage (Deuteronomy 11:13), written on one side, and on the other side, the name of God.

The commandment to place *mezuzot* on the doorposts of Jewish homes comes from Deuteronomy 6:4-9. In that passage, God commands his followers to keep his words constantly in their minds and hearts and to write them on the doorposts of their houses.

The scroll must be handwritten in a special style of writing and the case with the scroll in it is fitted to the right-side doorpost on an angle. The *mezuzah* is a constant reminder of God's presence and his commandments. Every time a Jew passes through a door with a *mezuzah* on it, he touches the *mezuzah* and then kisses the fingers that touched it, to express his love for God and respect for God's commandments.

Tefillin (phylacteries)

The *Shema* orders Jews to bind God's commandments to their hands and between their eyes. Jews therefore bind to their arms and foreheads a leather pouch (*tefillin*) containing scrolls of *Torah* passages.

Like the *mezuzah*, *tefillin* remind Jews of God's commandments. At weekday morning services, one case is tied to the arm with leather straps extending down the arm to the hand. Then another case is tied to the head. The case on the forehead and the straps hang down over the shoulders.

Tzitzit and tallit

The *Torah* also commands Jews to wear *tzitzit* (fringes) at the corners of their garments as a reminder of God's commandments (Numbers 15:37-41). This commandment only applies to four-cornered garments which were common in biblical times. Jewish men commonly wear a special four-cornered garment, similar to a *poncho*, called a *tallit katan*. A four-cornered shawl, called a *tallit*, is worn by adult men during morning services, along with the *tefillin*.

Yarmulke

The Hebrew word for this head covering is *kippah*. It is an ancient practice for Jews to cover their heads during prayer as a sign of respect for God.

Magen David

Although relatively new, the *Magen David* (shield of David, or Star of David) is the symbol most commonly associated with Judaism today. It is supposed to represent the shape of King David's shield (or perhaps the emblem on it), but there is no support for that claim in any early rabbinic literature.

Today, the *Magen David* is a universally recognized symbol of Jewry. It appears on the flag of the state of Israel. The Israeli equivalent of the Red Cross is known as the Red Magen David.

Chai

This symbol, commonly seen on necklaces and other jewelry and ornaments, is the Hebrew word *chai* ("living"). Donations to charity are routinely given in multiples of 18 (the numeric value of the word *chai*).

Q: What does kosher food mean?

A: The Jews derive their dietary restrictions from instructions in the *Torah*.

Kashrut is the body of Jewish law dealing with the foods that Jews can and cannot eat along with the rules about cooking and eating these foods. *Kashrut* comes from the Hebrew root Kaf-Shin-Resh and means "fit," "proper" or "correct." It is the same root as the more commonly known word "kosher" which refers to food that meets these standards.

Food that is not kosher is commonly referred to as *treyf*. It means "torn" and is derived from the commandment not to eat animals that have been torn by other animals.

Q: What foods may not be eaten?

A: Jews can eat land mammals that have cloven hooves and chew the cud (Leviticus 11:3; Deuteronomy 14:6). The *Torah* specifies that the camel, the rock badger, the hare and the pig are not kosher because each lacks one of these

two qualifications. Sheep, cattle, goats and deer are kosher.

Only fish that have fins and scales may be eaten (Leviticus 11:9; Deuteronomy 14:9). Thus, shellfish such as lobsters, oysters, shrimp, clams and crabs are all forbidden, but fish like tuna, trout, salmon and herring are permitted.

All birds of prey or scavengers are forbidden birds, but other birds, such as chicken, geese, ducks and turkeys are permitted.

The prohibition on eating forbidden foods includes the eggs from these birds.

All winged insects are forbidden.

Grape products made by non-Jews may not be eaten.

Q: What constitutes a kosher kitchen?

A: Of the animals that may be eaten, the birds and mammals must be killed in accordance with Jewish law which stipulates that all blood must be drained from the meat or broiled out of it before the flesh is eaten. Meat should, therefore, be bought at a kosher butcher or be certified kosher.

On three occasions the *Torah* commands that a kid is not to be boiled in its mother's milk (Exodus 23:19; 34:26; Deuteronomy 14:21). The Oral Law explains that these passages prohibit eating meat and dairy foods together.

The separation of flesh and dairy produce includes not only the foods themselves, but the utensils, pots and pans with which they are cooked, the plates from which they are eaten, the dishwashers or bowls in which they are washed and the towels on which they are dried.

So a kosher household has at least two sets of pots, pans and dishes.

Fish, eggs, fruits, vegetables and grains can be eaten with either meat or dairy.

Q: Who are the famous and influential Jews?

"I believe that the Jews have made a contribution to the human condition out of all proportion to their numbers." *Peter Ustinov*

FAMOUS JEWS
BIBLE TIMES
Abraham, c. 20th-19th century BCE
Moses, 13th century BCE
King David, 1000 BCE
King Solomon, c. 990–c. 933 BCE
Hillel, c. 70 BCE–10 CE, theologian
Flavius Josephus, c. 38–c. 100 CE, historian
1ST TO 19TH CENTURIES, CE
Simon Bar Kokhba, 135, general
Maimonides, 1135–1204, theologian
Moses Mendelssohn, 1729–1786, philosopher
Mayer Rothschild, 1744–1812, financier
Heinrich Heine, 1797–1856, poet
Benjamin Disraeli, 1804–1881, politician
Felix Mendelssohn, 1809–1847, musician
20TH TO 21ST CENTURIES
Sigmund Freud, 1856–1936, psychiatrist
Gustav Mahler, 1860–1911, composer
Marcel Proust, 1871–1922, novelist
Harry Houdini, 1874–1926, magician
Albert Einstein, 1879–1955, physicist
David Ben-Gurion, 1886–1973, founder of Israel
Franz Kafka, 1883–1924, author
Boris Pasternak, 1890–1960, novelist, poet
Groucho Marx, 1890–1977, comedian
George Gershwin, 1898–1937, composer
Golda Meir, 1898–1978, prime minister of Israel
Leonard Bernstein, 1918–1990, musician
Isaac Bashevis Singer, 1904–1991, author
Henry Kissinger, b. 1923, politician
Anne Frank, 1929–1945, diarist
Steven Spielberg, b. 1947, film-maker

7 CONFUCIANISM AND TAOISM

The founder of Confucianism

Confucius

Confucianism originated in China. Its founder, Confucius, was born on August 27, 551 BCE in the feudal state of Lu, (modern Shandong province) in north China. He ranks as the greatest and most influential of Chinese philosophers. (Confucius died in 479 BCE.) His teachings held sway in China for over 20 centuries and until the beginning of the twentieth century Chinese civil service examinations were based on the thoughts of Confucius.

The teachings of Confucius are codes of conduct, but many question whether it can be called a religion. It does, however, contain within it a religious world view.

Sad personal life

Confucius did not enjoy a happy family life and his teachings were not appreciated by the rulers of China.

- He was an orphan.
- He was largely self-educated.
- He married when he was 19 years old, but his bride ran away from him.
- He held relatively minor governmental posts: Governor of Chung-tu, then minister of works, and minister of justice.
- In his own lifetime Confucius was not a powerful man, nor particularly famous.
- Confucius' teaching was rejected by the Chinese government.

Confucius' character

Confucius had many gifts. He loved poetry and music. He was renowned for his humility which is encapsulated in one of his sayings: "I never walk with two companions but I learn something."

China's turmoil

Chinese culture and civilization were many thousands of years in advance of that in the west. Even so, during Confucius' lifetime China was ravaged by the fighting and corruption of her own nobles. As a result China became weak and vulnerable, to attacks from outsiders. Confucius' own province was under attack 21 times in 200 years.

Confucius' solution

Confucius thought that the remedy to China's turmoil lay in training ministers of state to govern the different Chinese provinces. Thus, Confucius trained a group of young men in the art of good government in the hope that their skills would be called upon by the decadent nobles.

Confucius tried to find the best way to live in this world. He gave up his job as a school teacher in order to teach people how to live in peace and harmony.

Education, education, education

Confucius believed that society's evils would be cured if ignorance were stamped out. If people were correctly educated they would lead noble lives. This led him to make good education the first priority throughout the country.

Teachers

Teachers, he felt, should be the most important people in society, even more important than parents. As a result of Confucius' teaching, this became the prevailing view in China. At the imperial court each courtier and servant had to bow reverently to the Emperor. But the Emperor had to bow at the feet of his teacher who did not bow to the Emperor.

Confucius and God

Confucius emphasized that moral character was the source of social order. He did not teach about God; his concern was for things of this world and not of the next.

The golden rule

A person who wants to be properly treated when in a subordinate role must treat his own inferiors with propriety.

Confucius taught a negative version of the golden rule. "What you do not wish others to do to you, do not do to them." *Confucius*

Compare his with the golden rule of Christianity recorded in Luke 6:31. "[Jesus said] Do to others as you would have them do to you."

After Confucius' death his followers commemorated him by building temples. These temples may now be found throughout the Chinese empire.

Confucian beliefs

Confucius believed that the best way to lead a better life was by:

- respecting other people
- worshiping ancestors.

He taught that one's own well-being depended on the well-being of other people.

Jen (a sympathetic attitude)

Confucianism developed into a system of ethical precepts by which society could be run. It was based on the practice of *jen*, which has been variously defined as:

- sympathy
- loving-heartedness.

Confucius believed that people would become happy if they followed five virtues:

- kindness
- righteousness
- sobriety
- wisdom
- trustworthiness.

Jen means respect for life and showing courtesy and loyalty to other people at all times. The world becomes a more peaceful place when all people strive to be true gentlemen and gentlewomen. For the Confucian the ultimate goal of conduct and self-transformation is *jen*.

Li (proper behavior)

Correct conduct is the second foundation of Confucianism. Confucius believed that the practice of social etiquette and ritual, or *li*, was the quickest way to instil ethical growth. From early childhood he had been fascinated by rites and rituals and often praised the ceremonial observances of ancient China. *Li* consists of four basic ideas:

- moderation
- agreement of names with deeds
- the importance of family
- respect for age.

Moderation

Moderation enables people to live between life's extremes. Based on *I Ching* (the Taoist philosophy which describes all nature and human endeavor in terms of the interaction of *yin* and *yang*), Confucius taught that extremes always produce their opposites. The only way to maintain harmony and balance was to remain within limits. This brought happiness.

Agreement of names

Agreement of names means that everyone should behave in accordance with their name. So a father should act as a father and be a father, never neglecting his fatherly duties.

Confucius taught that people would fulfil their role in society if they did their duty.

Family, social relationships and old age

The family was crucially important to Confucius and he taught that people should love and honor their families.

Confucius taught that five social relationships had to be honored at all times:

- the master and servant relationship
- the father and son relationship
- the husband and wife relationship
- the relationship between elder and younger siblings
- the relationship between friends.

Confucius also taught that everyone should honor the elderly.

Worship of ancestors

Confucians worship their ancestors at the altars in their homes and in their temples.

"While parents are alive serve them according to *li*, the ritual; when they die bury them according to the ritual; and sacrifice to them according to the ritual."
Confucius, Analects 2:5

Confucian texts

Confucianism does not have any divinely inspired or revealed scripture. Its basic texts are divided into five different groupings known as the Five, Six, Nine, Twelve or Thirteen Classics.

Analects

The *Analects*, found in the Twelve and Thirteen Classics, contain the essence of Confucius' teaching. They were not written by Confucius himself but by his students, about 70 years after his death.

The word *Analects*, from the Greek work *analekta* means "selected things."

Sayings of Confucius

"A good person always seeks to help others to do good, not to do ill."
Confucius

"Tzu-Kung asked, saying, 'What would you feel about a man who was loved by all his fellow-villagers?'

The Master said, 'That is not good enough. Best of all would be that the good people in his village loved him and the bad hated him.'" *Analects 13:23-24*

"The essence of knowledge is, having it, to apply it; not having it, to confess your ignorance." *Analects, 2, 17*

F.A.Qs about Confucianism
Q: Where do followers of Confucius live today?

A: Most followers of Confucius live in the Far East: Japan, Korea, Singapore, Taiwan, and Taiwan.

It is particularly strong in South Korea and Taiwan where traditional Confucian education and shrines still prevail.

Q: How many followers of Confucius are there today?

A: Between four and five million. In the twentieth and twenty-first centuries Confucianism has been in decline.

The overthrow of the Chinese monarchy (1911), the adoption of communism as the state ideology of China under Mao Zedong (1893–1976) and today's materialistic and acquisitive society have all contributed to the erosion of the influence of China's greatest philosopher.

Taoism: its history and beliefs

Lao Tze

The philosopher Lao Tze (or Lao Tzu), the founder of Taoism (pronounced Dowism) and a contemporary of Confucius, made a lasting impact on China at about the same time as Buddha was teaching his followers in India.

Very few details are known about the life of Lao Tze. Indeed, it is not known for certain that he ever existed. Lao Tze (Chinese for "old person" or "old philosopher") is said to have been born around 604 BCE. According to legend he was born with white hair, aged 72 years old, and so was given the nickname Lao Tzu (meaning "Old Boy"). Also according to legend Lao Tze was a royal librarian named Li Erh and he is traditionally held to be the author of the *Tao Te Ching* – the central text of Taoism.

The rise and decline of Taoism

Taoism started as a combination of psychology and philosophy but by 440 CE it had evolved into something more akin to a religious faith. It was then adopted as a state religion in China and Lao Tze became popularly venerated as a deity. Taoism, along with Buddhism and Confucianism, became one of the three great religions of China.

With the end of the Ch'ing Dynasty in 1911, state support for Taoism ended. Much of the Taoist heritage was then destroyed under the rule of the war lords.

When the Communists gained power in 1949, religious freedom was so severely restricted that by 1960 the several million Taoist monks were reduced to fewer than 50,000.

During the cultural revolution in China, 1966–1976, much of the remaining Taoist heritage was destroyed.

From 1982, under Deng Xiao-ping, some religious tolerance was restored.

Teaching of Lao Tze

Lao Tze, known as the Supreme Master, taught that a creative spiritual force underlies the universe, flows through all things, and lies behind the scenes of all human life. He called this force the Way or *Tao* ("path").

Goal of Taoism

Taoists aim to become one with *Tao*. In this life, this brings liberation to the soul. Taoists seek to find a potion (elixir) that will make them immortal and give them eternal life. Meditating on waterfalls, lakes, trees and mountains is thought to be especially conducive to achieving the goal of living in harmony with the natural world.

Lao Tze and God

Lao Tze taught that only *Tao* existed and there were no such beings as gods and goddesses. So there is no God to hear Taoists' prayers or to act on them. Therefore, Taoists seek answers to life's problems through inner meditation and outer observation.

But the followers of Lao Tze worshiped him as well as other leading Taoist teachers.

Taoists also worship the sun, moon, stars, and tides.

Key beliefs

The good or evil acts a person engages in during his lifetime determine the fate of his soul.

Development of virtue is one's chief task. The three "jewels" to be sought are:

- compassion
- moderation
- humility.

Taoists believe that people are good by nature. So if you are kind to others such treatment will probably be reciprocated.

Tai Chi

Taoists seek to control their mental states and their physical actions by means of a series of exercises known as *Tai Chi* (Chinese [Mandarin] "shadow boxing") which are designed to aid meditation, provide self-defense and bring about healing.

Traditional Chinese medicine teaches that illness is caused by blockages or lack of balance in the body's "chi" (intrinsic energy). *Tai Chi* is believed to balance this energy flow.

It consists of a series of slow deliberate movements which massage the body's internal organs and so enhance their functions. It is believed that *Tai Chi*:

- stimulates the central nervous system
- lowers blood pressure
- improves the circulation

of the blood
- relieves stress
- gently tones muscles
- enhances digestion.

Five don'ts

In its teaching about how to live Taoism forbids:

1. lying
2. stealing
3. adultery
4. consuming alcohol
5. murder.

Good deeds

Taoists seek to develop virtue and show compassion, moderation and humility on all occasions. The believe they should:

- obey their elders
- be tolerant
- be loving to their parents
- assist other people
- acts in selfless ways.

Festivals

Zhon-gyual is the most important Taoist festival. It is celebrated on the fifteenth day of the seventh month. This is the time when the hungry souls of the dead are supposed to appear in the world of the living. This enables Taoist priests to free them from their suffering.

Jiao

The most important Taoist rite, *Jiao*, drives evil spirits out of the ground and it is left pure.

Taoist writings

Taoist creed

"We believe in the formless and
eternal *Tao*, and we recognize all
personified deities as being mere
human constructs. We reject hatred,
intolerance and unnecessary violence,
and embrace harmony, love and
learning, as we are taught by Nature.
We place our trust and our lives in the
Tao, that we may live in peace and
balance with the Universe, both in this
mortal life and beyond." *Creed of the
Western Reform Taoist Congregation*

Tao-te-Ching

According to Taoist legend, Lao Tze
abandoned his job, rode off to the
mountains on the back of an ox where
the guardian of the mountain pass asked
him to write down his teachings. In this
way the sacred book of Taoism, *Tao-te-
Ching*, (or *Daodejing*, "The Way of
Power" or "The Book of the Way") came
into existence.

It describes an ideal human condition,
free from desire, which is achieved by
following the *Tao*.

"If you want to become whole, first let
yourself become broken. If you want
to become straight, first let yourself
become twisted. If you want to
become full, first let yourself become
empty. If you want to become new,
first let yourself become old. Those
whose desires are few get them, those
whose desires are great go astray."
Tao-te-Ching

"As to dwelling, live near the ground.
As to thinking, hold to that which is
simple. As to conflict, pursue fairness
and generosity. As to government, do
not attempt to control. As to work, do
what you like doing. As to family, be
fully present." *Tao-te-Ching*

"Regard your neibor's gain as your
gain and your neighbor's loss as your
loss" *Tai-shang Kang-ying P'ien*

F.A.Qs (Frequently Asked Questions) about Taoism

Q: What does the *yin* and *yang* symbol mean?

A: The symbol of Taoism represents *yin* and *yang* in balance.

According to a Chinese theory there are two forces in the world: *yin* and *yang*. *Yin* and *yang* symbolize pairs of opposites which may be seen throughout the universe. These opposites include good and evil, light and dark, male and female. The *yin* symbol represents the female, passive principle, while the *yang* represents the male, active principle. Together they are responsible for all of creation. According to this theory, wise people are able to discern forces in the seasons, in their food and elsewhere and regulate their lives accordingly.

Taoism claims to bring harmony to opposites, as there would be no love without hate, no light without dark, no male without female.

Q: Where do Taoists live today?

A: Taoists live in China, Japan, Hong Kong, Taiwan, Malaysia and Vietnam.

In 2000 CE Taoism had more than 20 million followers.

Q: What impact does Taoism have on North American culture?

A: Many ideas and practices that underlie "New Age" thinking and alternative medicine derive from Taoism. These include:

- acupuncture
- meditation
- herbalism
- martial arts
- holistic medicine.

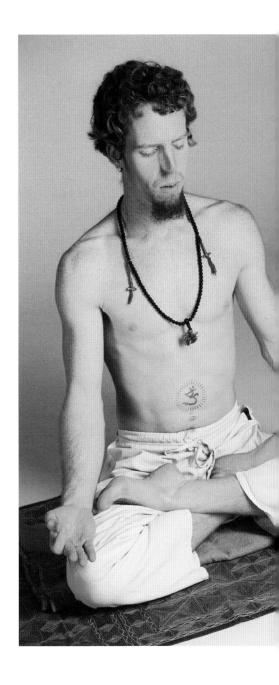

8 THE BAHA'I FAITH

CONTENTS	
	page

The Baha'i faith: its origin

Introduction

This religion, the youngest of the world's religions, was founded in 1863 in Iran.

It emphasizes the spiritual unity of all humankind.

The name

Baha'i comes from the Arabic word *bah* which means "splendor" or "glory."

Bab

On May 23, 1844, in Shiraz, Persia (now Iran), a young man, Mirza Ali Muhammed (1820–50), known as Bab (or the Bab, meaning "the Gate"), declared that God's messenger would shortly appear.

He believed that he was the latest spiritual leader. Infuriated with this claim, Muslim clergy executed him on July 9, 1850, in the public square of the city of Tabriz. Later, 20,000 of his followers were massacred throughout Persia.

A building known as the golden dome, overlooking the Bay of Haifa, Israel, also known as the Shrine of Bab, contains Bab's remains.

Heretics

In the eyes of traditional Muslims Baha'is are heretics. They have been constantly and cruelly persecuted, especially in Iran where the Baha'i faith is not even recognized as a minority religion. As a result, the children of Baha'i parents are denied birth certificates which in turn means that they are never able to prove their identity.

Baha'u'llah

Baha'u'llah, or Baha-Allah (Arabic for "the glory of God"), born as Mirza Husain Ali in Teheran (1817–92), a follower of Bab, is recognized as the founder of the Baha'i faith. In 1863 he declared that he himself was the manifestation of God whom Bab had predicted.

He sent letters to world rulers telling

them to unite in one harmonious world civilization and advising them to disarm and put their energies into pursuing world peace.

Abdu'l-Baha, son of Baha'u'llah

As Baha'u'llah's successor, Abdu'l-Baha declared that he alone could give the correct interpretation to his father's writings. The Baha'i world community united around Abdu'l-Baha's interpretations and elaborations of Baha'u'llah's writings.

Keeping it in the family

Abdu'l-Baha appointed his grandson, Shoghi Effendi Rabbani, to be guardian of the Baha'i faith and interpreter of its teachings. Shoghi Effendi was Guardian for 36 years, until he died in 1957. During this time he translated many of the writings of his grandfather and great-grandfather into English. He also established local and national Baha'i institutions.

Every five years representatives of the national Baha'i communities meet to elect the members of the Universal House of Justice, which administers the international affairs of the Baha'i faith.

Belief and action

Members of the Baha'i faith believe that humanity is a single people with a common destiny.

"The earth is but one country, and mankind its citizens." *Baha'u'llah*

Believing that the time for the

unification of the world in one global society has arrived, Baha'i communities work to break down prejudice and overcome the traditional barriers of race, class, creed and nation in order to promote the model of a global society.

Progressive revelation

Baha'u'llah believed that there is one God who progressively reveals his will to humankind. He taught that each of the great religions are stages in civilization's spiritual improvement. So Moses, Krishna, Buddha, Zoroaster, Jesus and Muhammad were all God's chosen messengers. Baha'u'llah also believed that God's identity needed to be retaught through a new prophecy to each successive generation.

The purpose of life

Baha'u'llah taught that each human being is "a mine rich in gems." The purpose of life on earth is to develop our human capabilities to benefit ourselves and humankind.

This is achieved through personal development by:

- daily prayer and meditation
- working with people of different social and ethnic backgrounds
- avoiding alcohol and cigarettes
- not speaking ill of other people
- supporting the family unit
- holding marriage in high esteem
- recognizing the equality of husband and wife
- using dialogue to solve problems.

The quest for global unification

Steps towards unification

Members of the Bahai'i community believe humanity has now come of age and will shortly be united. They seek to make this a reality by working for:

- the eradication of all forms of prejudice
- equal opportunities for women
- the recognition of religious truth in all religions
- the elimination of poverty and wealth
- global education
- the acceptance that each person needs to seek for truth
- the establishment of a worldwide commonwealth of nations
- recognition that all true religions are in harmony with reason and science.

Unity

For Baha'u'llah the goal of faith was the oneness of humankind, that is, the spiritual and organic unity of all races, nations and all mankind. He believes that unity between people and nations is necessary before global peace can be achieved.

"So powerful is the light of unity that it can illuminate the whole earth. We have come to unite and weld together all that dwell on earth." *Baha'u'llah*

"The well-being of mankind, its peace and security, are unattainable unless and until its unity is firmly established." *Baha'u'llah*

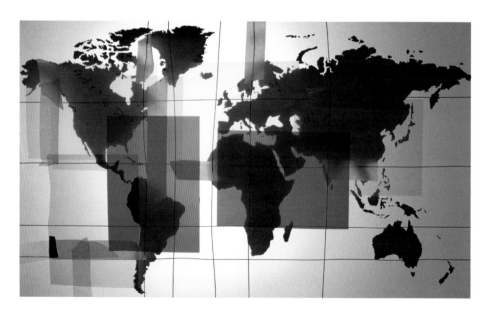

Steps to world unity

- A federation of nations.
- An international auxiliary language.
- The coordination of the world's economy.
- Universal education.
- A code of human rights for everyone.
- Integrated global communication.
- An international currency, weights and measures.

Links with the United Nations

Today the Baha'i faith actively supports the United Nations and the Baha'i International Community participates in United Nations consultations about:

- minority rights
- the status of women
- crime prevention
- control of narcotic drugs
- welfare of children and the family
- global disarmament.

Baha'u'llah's covenant

Members of the Baha'i faith claim that Baha'u'llah's covenant, unlike any previous religious system, sets out ways in which humanity can be welded together into an organic unity, based on spiritual principles. As Baha'u'llah's son, Abdu'l-Baha, put it, "So firm and mighty [is this covenant] that from the beginning of time until the present day, no religious dispensation has produced its like."

No clergy

The Baha'i faith does not have any clergy. They do not believe they need any priest or minister to help them. Baha'is believe that all people have the maturity to explore God's revelation for themselves through prayer, meditation, and consultation with others. To this end the Baha'i scriptures have been translated into over 800 different languages.

Supporting the Baha'i faith

The Baha'i faith is supported by voluntary contributions from its own members. No donations from outsiders are accepted.

Worship

Baha'i Houses of Worship are open to everyone. Each building has nine sides and a common central dome, symbolizing the diversity and essential oneness of the human race.

Devotions consist of prayers, meditations and readings from the sacred scriptures of the Baha'i faith, and from scriptures of other world religions.

Unaccompanied choirs provide music.

F.A.Q. about the Baha'i faith

Q: Where do members of the Baha'i faith live?

A: The Baha'i faith claims to be the second most widespread of the world's independent religions established in 189 independent countries and 46 territories.

Over 2,100 ethnic, racial and tribal groups belong to it and it has over 5 million members.

9 JAINISM

Jain beliefs

Introduction

Jainism originated in India. Like Buddhism, it is a reform movement which separated from Islam. It has an influence that is largely out of proportion to its size because of Mahatma Gandhi. Although he was not a Jain, he promoted Jainist teaching on non-violence (*ahimsa*).

Jain beliefs

1. Tirthankas

Jains worship 24 spiritual teachers, but they do not believe in a god. These teachers (*tirthankaras*) are their guides in life.

Mahavira is considered to be the 24th and most important *tirthankara*.

2. The universe

Jains believe in the cyclical nature of the universe, that is, our universe is without a beginning, without an end and without a creator.

3. Reincarnation

Jains believe in reincarnation, that is, that the soul is eternal and experiences many consecutive births in order to work toward complete enlightenment which ultimately leads to liberation (*moksa*). But for Jains the path to this liberation is different from that of Hindus and Buddhists. They teach that the path begins with *ahimsa* or non-

TIME-LINE	
BCE	
599	Mahavira ("Great Hero") is born into the *Kshatriya* (warrior) caste.
569	Leaves home to become an itinerant monk. He meditates and fasts as he searches for the truth.
557	Receives enlightenment and becomes a *tirthankara*. Devotes the rest of his life to teaching Jain enlightenment.
527	Dies, aged 72, with many followers, in western India.

harming. This means no harm must be done to any beings who have two, three, four or five senses; and for the ascetics it involves complete *ahimsa* for all creatures.

4. Karma

In common with Hinduism, Jains believe in the concept of *karma*, but in Jainism *karma* is more than a law of nature. It has substance and consists of fine particles of matter that stick to the soul.

Our souls collect this *karma*, either good *karma* (*punya*) or bad *karma* (*papa*). The state of one's *karma* ultimately determines one's ability to gain enlightenment.

5. The triple gems (*triratna*)

Jains can escape from the endless cycle of birth and rebirth by practicing the Three Jewels (*triratna*):

- **Right knowledge.** This comes from knowing the Jain creed.
- **Right faith.** This comes from believing the Jain creed.
- **Right conduct.** This comes from following the Jain creed.

In this way Jains are victorious over bondage to life's endless cycle of misery.

Jains and the soul

Jains believe that the soul (*jiva*) is eternal, uncreated, and infinite. It experiences countless rebirths until liberation (*moksa*) is finally achieved by gaining omniscience.

The enlightenment that leads to liberation is obtained by following or believing in the nine *tattvas*:

1. *jiva* (soul)
2. *ajiva* (non-soul)
3. *asrava* (our souls collect *karma*)
4. *papa* (bad *karma*)
5. *punya* (good *karma*)
6. *bandha* (the bondage of *karma* to the soul)
7. *samvara* (the stopping of collecting *papa*)
8. *nirjara* (getting rid of the bad *karma*)
9. *moksa* (complete liberation).

Elimination of suffering

Jains seek to eradicate suffering from the world. They teach that the primary causes of suffering and injustice in the world are:

- violence
- lack of compassion
- anger
- pride
- infatuation
- greed
- hatred
- craving.

Jain conduct

The Jain code of conduct

All Jains, but especially monks and nuns, aspire to keeping the five "great vows" of Jainism:

- chastity (*brahmacharya*)
- poverty, possessing nothing (*aparigraha*)
- telling the truth (*satya*)
- never stealing (*asteya*)
- practising non-violence (*ahimsa*).

Non-possessiveness

Attachment to material objects is the primary cause of bondage and leads to greed and jealousy which in turn leads to suffering and injustice

So Jains focus strongly on non-possessiveness toward material things (*aparigraha*), through: self-control, self-imposed penance, abstinence from over-indulgence and voluntary curtailment of one's needs.

Non-violence (*ahimsa*)

The distinctive principle of Jainism is non-violence (*ahimsa*) in both thought and action toward all living creatures. Jains teach that every living thing has a soul and so must not be harmed. This includes not only animals, plants and insects, but even microbes. To harm any creature, even accidentally, is very harmful for one's *karma*.

A phrase from a Jain holy text, the *Tattvartha Sutra*, explains this teaching: "*Parasparopagraho Jivanam*" (all life is mutually supportive).

Devout Jains wear masks to avoid accidentally swallowing any small flying insect. They will even sweep the ground before they walk on it just in case they should tread on an insect.

Vegetarianism

The practice of vegetarianism is motivated by compassion for living beings (*jiva daya*). Vegetarianism is a way of life for a Jain, being seen as integral to the practice of non-violence and peaceful coexistence.

Worship
Outside the temple

Jain temples (*basadi*) are ornate and beautiful reflecting the holiness of the sacred images which they house.

Inside the temple
1. *Tirthankaras*

Inside Jain temples there are statues of the 24 *tirthankaras* which are the focus of worship.

Jains stand in front of these statues and bow reverently to them. They then pour an offering over the statue. These offerings are one of the "five nectars":

- diluted milk
- yogurt
- butter
- sugar
- flowers.

They then clean the statues with pure water.

2. *Siddha cakra* (saint-wheel)

Jain temples have a saint-wheel consisting of representations of the Five Great Beings who sit in a meditative posture in a circle. The saint-wheel is invoked to help eradicate sin and promote goodness.

Two sects and nudity

By 82 CE Jainism had split into two principal sects: *Svetambara* (white-clad) and *Digambara* (sky-clad, space-clad or unclothed) who disagreed over the question of nudism.

Before he gained enlightenment, the Mahavira spent 12 years in complete austerity, fasting and praying. For the first 13 months of this period he wore only a loincloth. Then he took it off and was naked, not only for the remaining 11 years, but for the rest of his life.

1. *Digambara*

Digambara lived in the warmer zone of south India and believed that to become a saint, a man should abstain from:

- food
- possessions including clothing.

2. *Svetambara*

Svetambara lived in the cooler region to the north, the Shvetambara. They abandoned some of the ancient practices of Jainism and wore white robes.

Revered texts

The sacred texts of Jainism are the teachings of the 24 *tirthankaras* (the *Upangas*, spiritual teachers).

The word-for-word teaching of Mahavira was recorded in the sacred texts known as the *Purvas*. The 14 *Purvas* are agreed to be sacred texts by both the *Svetambara* and *Digambara* sects.

However, the *Svetambaras* also include:

- the *Angas* (rules for the ascetics, doctrine and narratives)
- the *Chedasutras* (disciplinary acts for ascetics)
- the *Mulasutras* (texts that contain the basic law)
- the *Prakirnakasutras* (hymns).

F.A.Qs about Jainism

Q: How many Jains are there?
A: About 4 million.

Q: Where do Jains live?
A: Mainly in India with large concentrations in Gujarat (western India bordering the Arabian sea).

There are about 75,000 Jains in the United States. The fastest growing population of Jains outside India is in Leicester, England, where over 16,000 Jains live.

Q: What work do Jains do?
A: The Jains are among the wealthiest people in India.

Most become businessmen as they are opposed to engaging in agriculture as this would involve them in harming animals.

Jains often use their wealth to make large donations toward the building of temples.

10 SHINTOISM

Teaching and beliefs

Introduction

The name "Shinto" (meaning "the way of the gods") was first used by Buddhist missionaries to describe the religion they found in Japan in the fifth century BCE.

Shinto is the native religion of Japan going back to ancient times. The origin of its beliefs and rituals are unknown.

1. *Kami*

Shinto teaches the existence of numerous spiritual beings and gods known as *kami*. This idea is derived from the animist belief that supernatural forces live in natural objects. Shinto followers believe that these spirits, or gods (*kami*) live in:

- animals
- plants
- natural places, such as rivers, mountains and paddy fields.

2. The divine emperors

The most important *kami* is the sun goddess – Amaterasu. It is believed that in the seventh century BCE, Amaterasu's son married the daughter of the god of Fuji-Yama (the snow-capped volcano of Japan) and that their grandson became the first emperor of Japan. All successive emperors are thought to have been divine.

3. Emperor worship

Until 1945 Japan held firmly to Emperor worship. More than 350 shrines were devoted to the Emperor. In the schools all children bowed before a picture of the Emperor. Children were taught to memorize the names of the past 124 emperors.

It was believed that anyone who was killed while fighting for the emperor at once became a god. Consequently, during World War II, many *kamikaze* Japanese pilots committed *hara-kiri* (originally a form of ritual suicide) by directing their bomb-laden planes into enemy targets. They preferred suicide to the shame of surrender.

End of state Shinto

After Japan was defeated in World War II Emperor Hirohito was forced to declare that:

- he was not divine
- the Japanese were not the master race in the world
- state Shinto, the national religion of Japan, had officially come to an end.

Shinto festivals

Every shrine has its own annual festival (*matsuri*) when worshipers visit the shrine to honor its *kami*.

During the festival portable shrines (*mikoshi*) are also paraded through the streets so everyone can benefit from the blessing of the *kami*.

Sacred places and sites

There are more than 80,000 shrines (*jinja*) to Shinto deities in Japan. Each one is dedicated to a particular *kami*. Japan's most important shrine, at Ise, is dedicated to Amaterasu.

Every 20 years tradition dictates that this shrine be completely destroyed and rebuilt on exactly the same site using new wood.

Japan's most sacred mountain is Mount Fuji. On its summit is a Shinto shrine which is visited by millions of pilgrims every year.

Visiting a Shinto shrine

At the heart of Shinto worship is the visit to the shrine. When visiting a shrine a worshiper passes under a wooden archway or gateway (*torii*) which serves as a buffer between the outside world and the sacred shrine. He then washes his hands at a water trough, as an act of purification, because he is now standing on holy ground. He hangs up wooden tablets with prayers written

on them and moves on through the first of two halls. The first hall of worship (*haiden*) is where many dances and religious ceremonies are held.

This leads him to the second hall (*honden*), usually a one-story building approached by broad steps. This second hall is the main hall and houses the shrine where the *kami* is said to live. His presence is symbolized by a sacred symbol such as a sword or mirror.

The worshiper does not enter the shrine itself but rings a bell to alert the god to his presence. He makes an offering of rice or money, bows twice, claps his hands twice, to welcome the *kami*, recites some sacred verses, says a prayer, bows once again and claps his hands again. Then he leaves.

Worshiping at home

Many people worship *kami* in their homes at small wooden shrines.

Little dogma

Shinto has very little systematic doctrine, but followers of Shinto are expected to:

- celebrate the *kami*
- support the societies which have the *kami* as their patrons
- remain pure and sincere.

F.A.Q about Shintoism

Q: How many followers of Shinto are there?

A: There are about 3.5 million followers of Shinto.

11 ZOROASTRIANISM (PARSIS)

Zoroastrian beliefs

Origins of Zoroastrianism

The origins of Zoroastrianism can be traced back over 3,000 years to ancient Persia. Although Zoroastrianism originated in Persia (Iran) when Iran became a Muslim country in the ninth century CE, some of its followers fled to India where they were allowed to live in peace. Those who remained in Iran have always been harshly persecuted.

Zoroaster

The dates of Zoroaster are disputed, ranging from 600 BCE to 1,500 BCE. If the latter is accurate, then Zoroaster would have been the first of the great prophets of the world's religions.

Zoroaster only appears as an historical figure in the early part of the Zoroastrian scriptures. As a local Persian chieftain he is supposed to have struggled against Turanian aggressors in his battle to found a holy agricultural state.

Zoroastrian scriptures

The Zoroastrian scriptures, the *Avesta*, were thought to be so sacred that they were not written down. Instead they were passed on from one generation to the next by word of mouth. It was eventually committed to writing during the tenth century BCE in the Pahlavi language, a Middle Persian language.

The *Avesta* includes a series of poems, the *Gathas*, not dissimilar to the hymns of the Vedas, which may go back to Zoroaster himself. They form the basis of a liturgy which is used to ward off evil spirits.

Zoroastrian beliefs

1. God

The name of the one God is *Ahura Mazda* (the Wise Lord). He is the creator of the world, but he is also a personal God and a friend of not only Zoroastrians, but of all people.

Zoroastrians sometimes refer to their religion as "The Good Religion" as they believe in a good God who created a good world in which men and women are devoid of any original sin.

2. The evil spirit

Ahura Mazda is opposed by the evil spirit *Angra Mainyu* (Destructive Spirit) who will eventually be defeated by the forces of good.

3. Lesser gods

The six lesser gods of Zoroastrianism are called *Amesha Spentas*.

4. Zoroaster

Zoroaster taught that one day a savior (*Saoshyant*) will come and evil will be wiped out and the world will be perfect.

This savior will be born of a virgin. When he comes the dead will be resurrected.

5. Two judgments

After death people are judged according to how they have lived. Those who have done more good than evil are allowed to cross the Bridge of the Separator (Chinvat Bridge) into heaven. But those who have done more evil than good fall from the Chinvat Bridge into the abyss of hell.

A second judgment takes place after the resurrection.

Worship and sacred fire

Zoroastrians worship in temples known as fire temples. Sacred fire, representing truth and righteousness, is the focus of Zoroastrian worship.

Every temple has a fire altar which is kept burning and tended by priests. Zoroastrians pray in front of a source of light five times each day, tying and untying their sacred woollen belts (kustis) as they pray. Special services are held in the temple for weddings, funerals and for the receiving of kustis.

No cremation, no burial

Zoroastrians do not bury or cremate their dead because they think that the earth would be polluted by decaying dead matter. Instead, they place dead bodies in Towers of Silence (dakhma, circular stone towers) which are open to the sky. This practice allows vultures and other birds of prey to consume the dead bodies.

Throughout their lives Zoroastrians wear a sudreh (white undershirt). These sacred shirts are worn to symbolize the constant battle that has to be fought against evil.

The sudreh, as well as the kustris are laid on a white sheet on the top of the dead body.

No need to convert others

Zoroastrians believe that the righteous of every religion go to heaven. Since they consider all religions to be equal it is unnecessary to seek to convert other people to their faith.

They rely on marriage between Zoroastrians to increase their numbers.

F.A.Qs

Q: How many Zoroastrians are there today?

A: About 200,000.

Q: What is the link between Parsis and Zoroastrians?

A: Followers of Zoroastrianism who live in west India are known as Parsis. The word Parsis is derived from the word "Persia" from where they migrated to escape persecution in the eighth century CE.

By far the majority of Zoroastrians live in India, and fewer than 10,000 are left in Iran.

Today, Zoroastrians are often called by the name of Parsis.

12 THE PRIMAL RELIGIONS

The primal religions: Australasia

World of the spirits

In areas where people rely directly on nature for their food and survival, the natural world is often revered and even feared. Often, the beliefs of these peoples are focused on the worship of spirits. These spirits are thought to reside in trees, in the landscape and in animals.

Such religions are called primal religions or spirit religions.

Australasia

The peoples of the islands of the South Pacific, New Zealand and Australia each have their own myths (religious stories) to explain the origin and problems of the world.

The Australian Aborigines and Dreamtime

The religion of the Aborigines of Australia is based on the concept of Dreamtime. Long ago, it is said, supernatural beings called Ancestors roamed across Australia. They shaped the landscape and created the various forms of life, including the first human beings.

This mythical period of time is known as "Dreamtime."

These ancestral beings are known as kangaroo-men, emu-men, fig-men and bowerbird-women. Their footprints made the caves, hills, waterholes and other features of the landscape.

Aborigines believe that the earth is still sacred and must be carefully looked after and that they themselves are part of the earth and the earth is part of them.

By means of rituals known as "corroborees" in which they re-enact the myths of Dreamtime in their dances and songs, the people believe that they tap into its sacred power.

Maori myths

According to the Maoris of New Zealand, the islands of the South Pacific were brought up from the depths of the sea by the ocean spirit, Maui. While Maui was fishing he thought that he had caught a giant fish. Instead he hauled up the islands under the mistaken impression that he was catching fish.

The Maoris also have a myth which accounts for the rain. Ranginui and Papatuanuku, their first parents, were inseparable. However, one of their sons, Tane, eventually managed to pry them apart. Rangi (Sky Father) became the sky and Papa (Earth Mother) became the earth. The rain and mists are formed as they grieve at their separation.

Maoris believe that everyone returns to Mother Earth at death. They hold that the natural world is sacred. For this reason possession of land is of paramount importance. Those who possess land belong to their ancestors and to their living tribe, while those who have no land belong to nobody and are deemed to be worthless.

Melanesia

The islanders of the South Pacific live in awe of the sea which surrounds them and from which they derive their livelihood. Most of the gods they worship are spirits of the sea. Among their most important gods are the shark gods which they believe guard their islands. Dekuwaqa, the Fijian god of fishing, is in the form of a huge basking shark.

In addition to these ancestral cults, snake cults and totemism can still be found in Fiji. (see page 168)

Papua New Guinea

In the Southern Highlands of Papua New Guinea, the tribal religion is known as the "Foe," and its chief spirit is "Old One who is in the East." It is believed that with their powders, potions and spells, they can inflict disease and death on unwitting victims.

The primal religions: North America

Most primal religions of North America teach belief in a supreme being (named the Great Spirit) who created the earth.

Native Americans

The title "native American" refers to the indigenous people of North America. Native Americans, previously referred to as Indians, believe:

- that all life is sacred;
- that everything on earth has a spirit;
- that this spirit may be either good or evil;
- that the spirits of nature control what happens on earth each day.

The spirit of thunder is a great eagle known as the Thunderbird. Thunder comes from its beating wings and lightning from its eyes. It is thought of as good spirit as it produces rain for the crops and fights evil spirits.

Totem poles

The word "totem" comes from the North American Indian word for "relative." It is believed that each tribe is powerfully linked to a living creature, sharing its nature and under its protection. A totem pole is a tall decorated post on which each tribe carves the shape of its guardian spirit.

Inuit

The Inuit (Eskimos) of Canada, Greenland and Northern Alaska survive by successfully hunting animals, such as polar bears, whales and seals. They believe that each animal has the spirit of a god. Each time an animal is killed they celebrate the event with dancing and giving thanks to its spirit for providing them with meat and skins.

The *shaman* (witch doctors) of the Inuit peoples have the power to go into trances as they beat special drums. Once in a trance they are said to travel in the spirit world.

PRAYER

O Thou great mystery

Creator of the universe

Good and powerful as Thou art

Whose powers are displayed in

The wonders of the sun and the glories of the moon.

And the great foliage of the forest

And the great waters of the deep,

Sign of the four winds;

Whatever four corners of the earth that we may meet –

Let us be friends, pale face and red man,

And when we come to the end of that long trail,

And we step off into the happy hunting ground,

From which no hunter ever returns,

Let us not only have faith in Thee - O Thou great mystery -

But faith in each other, O thou Great Kitchin Manitou, hear us!

Chief Joseph Strongwolf, Nez Perce, c. 1840-1904

The primal religions: Africa

Spirit religions

Although many Africans are Christians or Muslims, many others are still devotees of the traditional spirit religions of their own countries. Though differing in their details, these religions have some common beliefs:

The Great God

The world was created by the Great God.

Lesser gods

There are a large number of lesser gods, such as, the the god of rivers, the god of rain and the god of thunder.

Spirits of nature

As every natural object is believed to possess its own spirit, there are hundreds and hundreds of such spirits, called "spirits of nature."

Spirits of ancestors

It is believed that their dead ancestors still live among the living in the form of spirits.

Ale – Nigeria's earth goddess

The Ibo people of Nigeria believe in an earth goddess named Ale. She helps the crops to grow and grants protection to her worshipers.

The witch doctor

The witch doctor still has an important role in traditional African communities producing healing medicines from his large store of plants, roots and berries.

People who are possessed by evil spirits are brought to the witch doctor to be exorcized.

Witch doctors are also called on to bless gatherings on state occasions and to ward off evil spirits.

Masks (called "passport" masks)

It is believed that each animal possesses a powerful spirit which lives in its head. Wooden spirit masks fashioned in the likeness of animals are thought to make them strong and protect them from evil. These masks, called "passport" masks, are worn when casting spells, and during religious dances, rites and rituals.

Fetishes

Any object which is believed to have magical or spiritual powers is known as a fetish. Some tribes practice cult worship of fetishes.

Some spirits have such control over certain fetishes that the person who has the fetish is thought to be controlled by the spirit; he is said to carry out its will. For this reason a fetish with great power is often declared taboo.

Dancing

It is believed that good spirits bring good, though they may bring evil, such as illness. In order to exorcize evil and cure ill people, complicated and energetic ritual dances are performed.

The primal religions: South America

In South America the people of the rainforests live in awe of the trees and forest animals. They believe that these plants and animals are very powerful spirits.

The jaguar

The jaguar, the fastest animal of the jungle and most feared hunter, is said to be the most powerful animal spirit.

The witch doctor (*shaman*) is believed to be endued with amazing powers that enable him to be transformed into a jaguar and visit the spirit world. To go in this power he may dress in jaguar skins and wear a necklace made of jaguar teeth.

When he is in a trance and visiting the animal world, the *shaman* asks for special favors from the animal spirits. Such requests are usually for somebody's health or for animals to hunt.

Ceremonial dances

Rainforest people believe that spirits can be summoned by means of ceremonial music and dances. The dancers put on traditional costumes and carefully paint their faces with plant dye. Dressed and decorated, they dance to the music of bamboo flutes, shell whistles and reed pipes, believing that as they dance they will be given magical powers.

When a person dies, singing and dancing ceremonies take place in order to speed the soul to the afterlife.

The people of the Andes

1. Pachamama

These mountain people believe that Pachamama, the Earth Mother, gives and sustains life.

2. The Apus

They believe that all things are controlled by the "Apus" who live in the high snow-capped peaks.

3. The Aukis

The "Aukis" are less powerful spirits who control the lower hills.

Each of the Apus and Aukis is named after a mountain or hill. These are the chief gods of the Indians of Colombia, Ecuador, Peru, Bolivia and Chile.

Along with Pachamama, the Apus and Aukis are thought to be responsible for making crops grow, keeping animals fertile and for looking after the community. To ensure that they are not hungry, angry or neglected, they offer drink-offerings, offerings of crops and, in some instances, animal sacrifices.

SYMBOLS OF THE WORLD'S RELIGIONS

THE STAR OF DAVID

The Star of David, a six-pointed star, is the best known symbol of Judaism. It is the symbol on the Jewish flag which is in great evidence in Jerusalem.

BUDDHIST WHEEL

The Buddhist wheel with its eight spokes is called the Wheel of Life. It stands for the central Buddhist teaching contained in the Noble Eightfold Path.

THE CROSS

The cross is the symbol of Christianity. It stands for the death of Jesus Christ who Christians believe was crucified in order to bring about the salvation of humankind.

THE SIKH SYMBOL

Ek-Onkar is the name given to the Sikh symbol. It represents the One God in whom Sikhs believe.

THE STAR AND CRESCENT MOON

The symbols of Islam are the star and crescent moon. They are the symbols on flags in Islamic countries.

CONFUCIANISM

The Chinese character for China is often used by Confucianism as its symbol, since it is the ancient religion of China.

THE HINDU SYMBOL

The Hindu symbol represents the sound Om which is sacred to the Hindus. It is said to contain the secrets of the universe and is often used as a chant in Hindu prayers.

TAOIST *YIN* AND *YANG*

The *yin* and *yang* symbol, representing the opposing yet complementary forces of nature, is the symbol of Taoism. It is also sometimes used by Confucianists.

JAINISM

Jainism's symbol is a wheel placed inside the palm of a hand. It stands for the cycle of birth and death in which everyone takes part.

THE GATE OF SHINTOISM

The symbol of Shintoism is the symbol for an entrance to a Shinto shrine – a torii gate.

ZOROASTRIANISM

The sacred fire is the focus of Zoroastrian worship. The fire represents righteousness and truth. It is kept burning in homes and temples.

ZEN BUDDHISM

The lotus flower is the symbol in Zen Buddhism. It stands for purity and goodness.

13 NEW AGE

Origin of the New Age Movement (NAM)

According to Rudyard Kipling, "East is East, and West is West, and never the twain shall meet." This is no longer true. For the NAM has been responsible for many Americans embracing pantheistic Eastern philosophy.

Its roots

The roots of the NAM may be traced to many sources: astrology, channeling, Hinduism, Gnostic traditions, spiritualism, Taosim, theosophy and Wicca. (Wicca is an old English word for necromancy, an ancient pagan natural religion enjoying a great revival in the past 50 years.)

1960s

1. The United Kingdom

In the United Kingdom this movement goes back to small groups which sprang up in the 1960s. In 1965, in Inverness,

Scotland, Eileen and Peter Caddy founded a seminal group known as the Findhorn Community. Those who belong to this community believe the spirits control the natural world and communicate to the everyday world through members of the community. When they meet together to worship, they dance, pray and meditate.

2. The USA

During the 1960s many people began to question the relevance of established traditions and values. The Peace Movement of the 1960s was highly critical of traditional attitudes to war.

There were radical movements in the realms of the environment and feminism. Many people began to look for answers in Eastern religions. Throughout the USA, but especially on the West coast, small groups were formed to enable enquirers to explore the ferment of ideas and test out these teachings. The ideas caught on and infiltrated most major religious and secular institutions.

1970s
The movement quickly became international. Its teaching filled a vacuum left by what many saw as the failure of Christianity and secular Humanism to provide spiritual and ethical guidance for the future.

A milepost in the development of the NAM was a "New Age Seminar" run by the Association for Research and Enlightenment, along with the establishment of the East-West Journal in 1971.

1980s and 1990s
During the 1980s and 90s, the movement became so established that it is now recognized as a major force in North American religion.

Definitions
Beyond a simple definition
The New Age Movement is beyond a simple definition as it is unlike other formal religions. It has:

- no holy text
- no central organization
- no list of members
- no clergy
- no geographic center
- no dogma
- no creed.

Some of the terms and definitions used by the NAM are mutually exclusive.

The NAM is a free-flowing spiritual movement with a network of believers who have broadly similar beliefs and practices.

NAM beliefs are often added to other formal religious beliefs.

NAM is "an extremely large, loosely structured network of organizations and individuals bound together by: common values (based on mysticism and monism – the world view that 'all is one') and common vision (a coming 'new age' of peace and mass enlightenment, the 'Age of Aquarius')." *Elliot Miller's A Crash Course on the New Age Movement*

Defining New Agers
New Agers "see themselves as advanced in consciousness, rejecting Judeo-Christian values and the Bible in favor of Oriental philosophies and religion." *Walter Martin, The New Age Cult*

Unity, but no dogma

"The New Age movement imposes no dogmas, but points toward the source of unity beyond all differences. [It supports:]
- devotion to truth,
- love for all living things,
- commitment to a life without personal judgment of others."
Jack Schafer, President and General Manager of NewAgeInfo.com

New Age beliefs

New Age beliefs are not written down in any one creed so it is not easy to codify them.

Six distinctive beliefs

According to Douglas R. Groothuis of Probe Ministries, it is possible to see six distinctive New Age beliefs:

- all is One
- all is God
- humanity is God
- a change in consciousness
- all religions are one
- cosmic evolutionary optimism.

14 doctrines

Norman L. Geisler has pinpointed 14 doctrines which he claims are typical of New Age religions:

1. An impersonal god (force).
2. An eternal universe.
3. An illusory nature of matter.
4. A cyclical nature of life.
5. The necessity of reincarnations.
6. The evolution of humankind into godhood.
7. Continuing revelations from beings beyond the world.
8. The identity of humankind with God.
9. The need for meditation (or other consciousness-changing techniques).
10. Occult practices (astrology and mediums).
11. Vegetarianism and holistic health.
12. Pacifism (or anti-war activities).
13. One world (global) order.
14. Syncretism (unity of all religions).

The NAM and belief in...

1. The NAM and belief in the source of authority

New Agers do not claim any external source of authority. Instead, they look to an internal source of authority – "the god within." The individual is the standard of truth. As Shirley MacLaine put it, "Truth as an objective reality simply does not exist."

2. The NAM and belief in God

New Agers believe that God is the Creator, but that he is part of (rather than separate from) his creation. New Agers do not seek God as revealed in a sacred text or as existing in a remote heaven; they seek God within self and throughout the entire universe. They believe that within each person there is a divine spark.

To New Agers God is not a Person, but is an impersonal force (similar to "the Force" popularized in the *Star Wars* trilogy of films).

3. The NAM and belief in Jesus Christ

New Agers deny that Jesus Christ was God, but are happy to say that he was a wonderful, spiritual teacher. They believe that the "Christ ideal," or spirit, dwelt in Hercules, Hermes, Rama, Mithra, Krishna and Buddha. Shirley MacLaine has claimed that Jesus is simply one of many great spiritual masters who have succeeded in tapping into their own godhood.

4. The NAM and belief in sin and salvation

Salvation is thought to be a more complete unity with the One – that is, with the Force or the impersonal presence. New Agers do not believe in the concept of sin so have no need for any doctrine of forgiveness.

5. The NAM and belief in the future life

Most New Agers believe in some form of reincarnation. In its classic form, the cycles of birth, death and reincarnation are necessary so that bad *karma* may be transformed until perfection is attained.

The Western version of reincarnation held by many New Agers places much less emphasis on bad *karma* but focuses on the upward spiral towards perfection through reincarnation. This belief in reincarnation has led to belief in the power and importance of "spirit guides" or "channels," that is, people who allow spirits from another dimension to speak through their bodies.

Pick and Mix

Shop around

New Age followers are encouraged to shop around for the beliefs that suit them. They may chose a combination of the following ideas:

Monism

All that exists is derived from a single source of divine energy.

Pantheism

All that exists is God; God is all that exists. This leads naturally to the concept of the divinity of the individual – that we are all gods.

Reincarnation

After death, each person is reborn and lives again as a human being. This cycle repeats itself many times. On ABC TV's *One On One* Shirley MacLaine said, "I'm convinced that I've lived before."

Karma

The good and bad deeds done in this life add and subtract from each person's accumulated record – the *karma*. At the end of this life, according to their *karma*, people are reincarnated into either a painful or a good new life. This belief is linked to reincarnation and both ideas are derived from Hinduism.

Aura

An aura is believed to be an energy field radiated by the body. Invisible to most people, it can be detected by some as a shimmering, multi-colored field surrounding the body. Those skilled in detecting and interpreting auras can diagnoze an individual's state of mind, and their spiritual and physical health.

Personal transformation

A profoundly intense mystical experience will lead to the acceptance and use of New Age beliefs and practices. Guided imagery, hypnosis, meditation and (sometimes) the use of hallucinogenic drugs are useful to bring about and enhance this transformation. Believers hope to develop new potentials within themselves:

- the ability to heal themselves and others;
- psychic powers;
- a new understanding of the workings of the universe.

Ecological responsibility

A belief in the importance of uniting to preserve the health of the earth which is often looked upon as Gaia (Mother Earth), a living entity.

Universal religion

If all is God, then only one reality exists and all religions are simply different paths to that ultimate reality. The universal religion can be visualized as a mountain with many *sadhanas* (spiritual paths) to the summit. There is no one correct path because all paths eventually reach the top. New Agers anticipate that a new universal religion incorporating elements of all current faiths will evolve and become accepted throughout the world.

New world order

As the Age of Aquarius unfolds, a New Age will develop. This will be a utopia in which there will be one world government and an end to wars, disease, hunger, pollution and poverty. In this new world, racial, religious and sexist and all other forms of discrimination will cease. People's allegiance to their tribe or nation will be replaced by a concern for the entire world and its people.

Support for NAM in USA

At the turn of the millennium it was estimated that out of the population of the USA:

- 8% believe in astrology as a method of foretelling the future;
- 7% believe that crystals are a source of healing or energizing power;
- 9% believe that tarot cards are a reliable base for life decisions;
- 25% believe in a non-traditional concept of the nature of God;
- 11% believe that God is "a state of higher consciousness that a person

  may reach;"
- 8% are happy to define God as "the total realization of personal, human potential;"
- 3% believe that each person is god.

Some surveys claim that New Agers represent 20% of the U.S. population.

NAM and theosophy

It is not easy to disentangle the numerous religious and philosophical threads that have been woven into New Age thinking. One influential thought-form is theosophy, founded in 1875. The theosophical world view teaches:

1. The universe and all that exists within it are one interdependent whole.
2. Every existent being – from atom to galaxy – is rooted in the same universal, life-creating and all-pervasive reality.
3. Recognition of the unique value of every living being expresses itself in: reverence for life, compassion for all, sympathy with the need of individuals to find truth for themselves and respect for every religious tradition.
4. The importance of promoting understanding and fellowship among people of all races, nationalities, philosophies and religions. All people, whatever their race, creed, sex, caste or color, are invited to participate.

New Age practices

Many practices are common among New Agers:

The spirit world
Some New Age groups believe that they can tune into the spirit world and to the creative forces of the universe through the use of healing, astrology and crystals.

Holistic health
This is a collection of healing techniques which attempt to cure disorders in mind, body and spirit and to promote wholeness and balance in the individual. Examples are acupuncture, crystal healing, homeopathy, iridology, massage, various meditation methods, polarity therapy, psychic healing, therapeutic touch and reflexology.

Crystals
Crystals are materials which have their molecules arranged in a specific, highly ordered internal pattern. This pattern is reflected in the crystal's special external structure with flat symmetrical surfaces. Many common substances, from salt to sugar, from diamonds to quartz, form crystals. They can be shaped so that they will vibrate at a specific frequency and are widely used in radio communications and computing devices. New Agers believe that crystals possess healing energy which they can tap into. Crystals are said to reduce stress and promote personal growth.

Channeling
Channeling has been called a step up the occult ladder from mediums. Channels claim that their bodies are taken over by "entities" or spirits from another dimension.

A well-known channeler, J. Z. Knight, claims to be a channel for Ramtha, a 35,000-year-old male spirit who calls himself "The Enlightened One."

NAM and meditation

Many New Agers use meditation as a way of engaging with their true self or soul.

For New Agers, meditation means blanking out the mind and releasing oneself from conscious thinking. This process is often aided by repetitive chanting of a mantra or focusing on an object.

NAM and divination

New Agers use various techniques to foretell the future, including *I Ching*, pendulum movements, and tarot cards.

Astrology and the Age of Aquarius

Astrology is the study of the movements and positions of the stars and planets in the belief that they influence each person's personality and future.

The Age of Aquarius is a reference to the belief, based on astrology, that around the turn of the millennium humankind moved into an age in history when human consciousness would expand and acquire greater spiritual power. The earth is said to pass into a new sign of the zodiac approximately every 2,000 years.

New Agers closely associate the Age of Aquarius with the New Age Movement.

Human Potential Movement

The Human Potential Movement (also known as the Emotional Growth Movement) is a loosely connected network of people claiming to produce numerous beneficial results from a variety of therapeutic methods, including:

- growth center programs
- Gestalt therapy
- primal scream therapy
- Transactional Analysis
- transcendental meditation and yoga.

It is claimed that these methods result in:

- understanding the meaning of life
- spiritual growth
- personal growth
- financial success
- improvement in relationships
- healing, both physical and psychological
- peace, both personal and global
- stabilization of the environment.

The NAM and the occult

Many occult practices make up the so-called "ancient wisdom" which the NAM follows. Such practices include:

- channeling
- divination
- astrology
- consulting spirits of the dead
- tarot cards
- crystals
- palm reading
- ouija boards
- yoga
- transcendental meditation
- casting spells.

F.A.Qs (Frequently Asked Questions) about the New Age Movement

Q: If polls indicate that 70% of Americans claim to be "born again" Christians, how can the same polls say that 50% of Americans believe in reincarnation?
A: Some people identify with Christianity and other religions, but incorporate many New Age concepts into their faith.

Q: What is the orthodox, conservative Christian approach to the NAM?
A: The New Age Movement is "the most dangerous enemy of Christianity in the world today...more dangerous than secular humanism." *Norman L. Geisler, professor of Systematic Theology at Dallas Theological Seminary*

Q: What do Christians have against the NAM?
A: Christians say the NAM:

- draws people away from the Christian faith
- engages in pagan practices
- believes in ideas common to eastern world faiths, like reincarnation
- places too much trust in the goodness of humankind
- denies the Trinity and a personal God.

Q: New Agers agree that Christ was a good teacher, so how are their beliefs faulty here?
A: New Agers marginalize Christ. The NAM does not deny Christ's existence but makes him one of a number of spiritual guides.

Q: Are there any famous people who have been associated with the movement?
A: Yes:

- Alice Bailey
- Fritjof Capra
- Norman Cousins
- Benjamin Creme
- John Denver
- Levi Dowling
- Marilyn Ferguson
- Barbara Marx Hubbard
- J. Z. Knight
- Norman Lear
- George Lucas
- Shirley MacLaine
- Abraham Maslow
- Ruth Montgomery
- Dr Barbara Ray
- Jeremy Rifkin
- David Spangler
- Alvin Toffler
- George Trevelyan.

Q: Does the NAM have any special symbols?
A: Yes, but the mere appearance of a New Age symbol does not necessarily mean that that person or group is associated with the New Age Movement.

Various symbols associated with the New Age are:

- butterfly
- concentric circles

- crescent moon
- eye in triangle
- goat head on pentagram
- pegasus (winged-horse)
- pyramid
- rainbow
- rays of light
- swastika
- triangle
- unicorn
- *yin-yang*.

Q: How many New Agers are there?
A: The NAM has:

- no central headquarters
- no leadership lists
- no membership lists.

However, it has been estimated that there are more than 60 million followers of various New Age practices and/or holders of one or more of the major beliefs of the New Age in the West.

14 *ATHEISTIC BELIEFS*

Atheism

Absence of belief

The word "atheism" means "without belief in god." Atheism is an absence of belief in the existence of gods or God or of any supernatural reality.

Many atheists will say that they have reached this position reluctantly, but add that intellectual honesty has forced them into this position. Atheists say that religion is a crutch for weak and gullible people.

"Religion...is the opium of the people." *Karl Marx*

"The first requisite for the happiness of the people is the abolition of religion." *Karl Marx*

Atheists maintain that they do not feel the need for such a crutch.

Reasons for unbelief

Those who are not able to believe in God cite some or all of the following reasons.

Science
There is no scientific evidence for God

When Uri Gagarin, on April 12, 1961, returned to earth after being the first person to orbit the earth in space, he declared that he had not observed any sign of God in space.

Yet, many scientists who do have Christian faith have rebutted atheism.

"In this modern world of ours many people seem to think that science has somehow made such religious ideas as immortality untimely or old fashioned. I think science has a real surprise for the skeptics. Science, for instance, tells us that nothing in nature, not even the tiniest particle, can disappear without a trace. Nature does not know extinction. All it knows is transformation. If God applies this fundamental principle to the most minute and insignificant parts of His universe, doesn't it make sense to assume that He applies it to the masterpiece of His creation, the human soul?" *Dr. Warner von Braun, founder of U.S. space exploration program*

"If I can't believe that the spacecraft I fly assembled itself, how can I believe that the universe assembled itself? I'm convinced only an intelligent God could have built a universe like this." *Jack Lousma, astronaut*

Jesus Christ reprimanded Thomas with the words, "Because you have seen me, you have believed; blessed are those who have not seen and yet have believed" (John 20:29).

Psychiatry

Some atheistic psychiatrists have pointed out that so-called experiences of God's presence have been explained by a clearer understanding of people's psychological needs and studies of the working of the brain.

Nietzsche said, "What was formerly contemplated and worshiped as God is now perceived to be something human." So he concluded: "What thinking man is there who still requires the hypothesis of a God?"

Sigmund Freud once said, "Devout believers are safeguarded in a high degree against the risk of certain neurotic illnesses; their acceptance of the universal neurosis spares them the task of constructing a personal one."

Responding to the claims of atheists, Francis A. Schaeffer once said, "Christianity believes that God has

created an external world that is really there; and because he is a reasonable God, one can expect to be able to find the order of the universe by reason."

Suffering

Some say it is inconceivable that a God could allow such suffering in the world he has made. Even when one takes away suffering caused by the nature of the planet (such as earthquakes and floods) and the use of free will, there still remains much suffering that a good God could surely prevent. So, concludes the hardened atheist, where is the evidence for a good and just God in our world which is "red in tooth and claw"?

"Man...
Who trusted God was love indeed
And love Creation's final law –
Though Nature, red in tooth and claw
With ravine, shrieked against his
creed." *Tennyson*

Christians do not claim to have all the answers, although writers like C. S. Lewis have pointed out that 99% of our suffering is due to man's inhumanity to man. In the face of suffering, Christians have often echoed the words of Job, "I know that my Redeemer lives, and that in the end he will stand upon the earth. And after my skin has been destroyed, yet in my flesh I will see God" (Job 19:25, 16).

Quotations for and against atheism

For atheism

"How am I, an a – temporal being imprisoned in time and space, to escape from my imprisonment, when I know that outside space and time lies nothing, and that I, in the ultimate depths of my reality, am nothing also."
Samuel Beckett

"The personality of God is nothing else that the projected personality of man." *Ludwig Feuerbach*

"All thinking men are atheists."
Ernest Hemingway

"That God does not exist, I cannot deny. That my whole being cries out for God I cannot forget." *Jean-Paul Satre*

Against atheism

"To be an atheist requires an infinitely greater measure of faith than to receive all the great truths which atheism would deny." *Joseph Addison*

"Atheism turns out to be too simple. If the whole universe has no meaning, we should never have found out that it has no meaning: just as, if there were no light in the universe and therefore no creatures with eyes, we should never know it was dark." *C. S. Lewis*

"We find the most terrible form of atheism, not in the militant and passionate struggle against the idea of God himself, but in the practical atheism of everyday living, in indifference and torpor. We often encounter these forms of atheism among those who are formally Christians." *Nicolai A. Berdyaev*

"Whoever considers the study of anatomy, I believe will never be an atheist; the frame of man's body, and coherence of his parts, being so strange and paradoxical, that I hold it to be the greatest miracle of nature."
Edward Herbert

"God never wrought a miracle to convince Atheism, because His ordinary works convince it." *Francis Bacon*

"I can see how it might be possible for a man to look down upon the earth and be an atheist, but I cannot conceive how he could look up into the heavens and say there is no God."
Abraham Lincoln

"All who seek God apart from Jesus Christ, and who rest in nature, either find no light to satisfy them, or form for themselves a means of knowing God and serving him without a Mediator. Thus they fall either into atheism or into deism. abhors."
Blaise Pascal

Communism and agnosticism

The Communist's argument

Communists say that communism came about because its first leaders were deeply concerned with the inequality and poverty of most ordinary people. They want a more equal society in which these injustices are remedied.

Communism is an atheistic worldview, akin to a religion in that it demands total commitment of the whole person. It has often been aggressive, seeking to force other people to its way of thinking.

Communism is often defined in terms of being an economic system or a form of government. The means by which it was prepared to achieve its ends have been adopted by some terrorists in the twentieth and twenty-first centuries.

"The one thing that Communists around the world must grasp is this: That freedom can only be gained through the barrel of a shotgun."
Mao Tse-Tung

"Patria o muerte!" ("Homeland or death!") *Fidel Castro*

Atheistic philosophy

At the heart of communism is its atheistic philosophy. Communism is not neutral on the question of religion; it is implacably opposed to it.

Christian opposition to atheism

Christians base their opposition to atheism on Psalm 14:1, "The fool says in his heart, 'There is no God.' They are corrupt, their deeds are vile; there is no one who does good."

Agnosticism

Agnosticism holds that the existence of God or gods cannot be proved.

The term "agnosticism" was coined by Professor T. H. Huxley at a meeting of the Metaphysical Society in 1876. He defined an agnostic as someone who believed that the question of whether a higher power existed was unsolved and insoluble.

The term agnostic also includes those who do not believe that the question is intrinsically unknowable, but instead believe that the evidence for or against God is inconclusive, and therefore are undecided about the issue.

"The Communists disdain to conceal their views and aims. They openly declare that their ends can be attained only by the forcible overthrow of all existing conditions. Let the ruling classes tremble at a communistic revolution. The proletarians have nothing to lose but their chains. They have a world to win.
WORKERS OF ALL COUNTRIES, UNITE!"
Karl Marx and Frederick Engels

Humanism

Who are their fellow-travelers?

Like Communism, humanism is not a
religion but an ideology. "Calling
Atheism a religion is like calling bald a
hair color." *Don Hirschberg*. For many
people in the twenty-first century
religion has been replaced by
commitment to an ideology. Fellow-
travelers with humanists are:

- atheists
- agnostics
- freethinkers
- rationalists
- skeptics.

Broadly speaking, humanists are people
who are interested in ethical living free
of religion.

The affirmations of humanism:
a Statement of Principles

"We are committed to the application of
reason and science to the understanding
of the universe and to the solving of
human problems.

We deplore efforts to denigrate human
intelligence, to seek to explain the world
in supernatural terms, and to look
outside nature for salvation.

We believe that scientific discovery
and technology can contribute to the
betterment of human life.

We believe in an open and pluralistic
society and that democracy is the best
guarantee of protecting human rights
from authoritarian elites and repressive
majorities.

We are committed to the principle of

the separation of church and state.

We cultivate the arts of negotiation
and compromise as a means of resolving
differences and achieving mutual
understanding.

We are concerned with securing
justice and fairness in society and with
eliminating discrimination and
intolerance.

We believe in supporting the
disadvantaged and the handicapped so
that they will be able to help themselves.

We attempt to transcend divisive
parochial loyalties based on race,
religion, gender, nationality, creed, class,
sexual orientation, or ethnicity, and
strive to work together for the common
good of humanity.

We want to protect and enhance the
earth, to preserve it for future
generations, and to avoid inflicting
needless suffering on other species.

We believe in enjoying life here and
now and in developing our creative
talents to their fullest.

We believe in the cultivation of moral
excellence.

We respect the right to privacy. Mature
adults should be allowed to fulfill their
aspirations, to express their sexual
preferences, to exercise reproductive
freedom, to have access to
comprehensive and informed health-
care, and to die with dignity.

We believe in the common moral
decencies: altruism, integrity, honesty,
truthfulness, responsibility. Humanist
ethics is amenable to critical, rational

guidance. There are normative standards that we discover together. Moral principles are tested by their consequences.

We are deeply concerned with the moral education of our children. We want to nourish reason and compassion.

We are engaged by the arts no less than by the sciences.

We are citizens of the universe and are excited by discoveries still to be made in the cosmos.

We are skeptical of untested claims to knowledge, and we are open to novel ideas and seek new departures in our thinking.

We believe in optimism rather than pessimism, hope rather than despair, learning in the place of dogma, truth instead of ignorance, joy rather than guilt or sin, tolerance in the place of fear, love instead of hatred, compassion over selfishness, beauty instead of ugliness, and reason rather than blind faith or irrationality." *Council for Secular Humanism*

Religious skepticism
"We are doubtful of traditional views of God and divinity"
"As secular humanists, we are generally skeptical about supernatural claims. We recognize the importance of religious experience: that experience redirects and gives meaning to the lives of human beings. We deny, however, that such experiences have anything to do with the supernatural. We are doubtful of

traditional views of God and divinity."
Paul Kurtz, Editor, Free Inquiry

"We reject the divinity of Jesus"
"However. we find that traditional views of the existence of God either are meaningless, have not yet been demonstrated to be true, or are tyrannically exploitative. Secular humanists may be agnostics, atheists, rationalists, or skeptics, but they find insufficient evidence for the claim that some divine purpose exists for the universe. They reject the idea that God has intervened miraculously in history or revealed himself to a chosen few or that he can save or redeem sinners. They believe that men and women are free and are responsible for their own destinies and that they cannot look toward some transcendent Being for salvation. We reject the divinity of Jesus." *Paul Kurtz, Editor, Free Inquiry*

"Religions have aroused morbid fear and dread"
"Religions are pervasive sociological phenomena, and religious myths have long persisted in human history. In spite of the fact that human beings have found religions to be uplifting and a source of solace, we do not find their theological claims to be true. Religions have made negative as well as positive contributions toward the development of human civilization. Although they have helped to build hospitals and schools and, at their best, have encouraged the

spirit of love and charity, many have also caused human suffering by being intolerant of those who did not accept their dogmas or creeds. Some religions have been fanatical and repressive, narrowing human hopes, limiting aspirations, and precipitating religious wars and violence. While religions have no doubt offered comfort to the bereaved and dying by holding forth the promise of an immortal life, they have also aroused morbid fear and dread. We have found no convincing evidence that there is a separable 'soul' or that it exists before birth or survives death. We must therefore conclude that the ethical life can be lived without the illusions of immortality or reincarnation. Human beings can develop the self confidence necessary to ameliorate the human condition and to lead meaningful, productive lives." *Paul Kurtz, Editor, Free Inquiry*

Will the secular humanists please stand up

"Although we who endorse this declaration may not agree with all its specific provisions, we nevertheless support its general purposes and direction and believe that it is important that they be enunciated and implemented. We call upon all men and women of good will who agree with us to join in helping to keep alive the commitment to the principles of free inquiry and the secular humanist outlook. We submit that the decline of

these values could have ominous implications for the future of civilization on this planet."

A Secular Humanist Declaration has been endorsed by the following individuals from the USA:

- George Abell (professor of astronomy, UCLA)
- John Anton (professor of philosophy, Emory University)
- Khoren Arisian (minister, First Unitarian Society of Minneapolis)
- Isaac Asimov (science fiction author)
- Paul Beattie (minister, All Souls Unitarian Church; president, Fellowship of Religious Humanism)
- H. James Birx (professor of anthropology and sociology, Canisius College)
- Brand Blanshard (professor emeritus of philosophy, Yale)
- Joseph L. Blau (Profelsor Emeritus of Religion, Columbia)
- Francis Crick (Nobel Prize Laureate, Salk Institute)
- Arthur Danto (professor of philosophy, Columbia University)
- Albert Ellis (executive director, Institute for Rational Emotive Therapy)
- Roy Fairfield (former professor of social science, Antioch)
- Herbert Feigl (professor emeritus of philosophy, University of Minnesota)
- Joseph Fletcher (theologian, University of Virginia Medical School)

- Sidney Hook (professor emeritus of philosophy, NYU, fellow at Hoover Institute)
- George Hourani (professor of philosophy, State University of New York at Buffalo)
- Walter Kaufmann (professor of philosophy, Princeton)
- Richard Kostelanetz (writer, artist, critic)
- Marvin Kohl (professor of philosophy, medical ethics, State University of New York at Fredonia)
- Paul Kurtz (Professor of Philosophy, State University of New York at Buffalo)
- Joseph Margolis (professor of philosophy, Temple University)
- Floyd Matson (professor of American Studies, University of Hawaii)
- Ernest Nagel (professor emeritus of philosophy, Columbia)
- Lee Nisbet (associate professor of philosophy, Medaille)
- George Olincy (lawyer)
- Virginia Olincy
- W. V. Quine (professor of philosophy, Harvard University)
- Robert Rimmer (novelist)
- Herbert Schapiro (Freedom from Religion Foundation)
- Herbert Schneider (professor emeritus of philosophy, Claremont College)
- B. F. Skinner (professor emeritus of psychology, Harvard)
- Gordon Stein (editor, *The American Rationalist*)
- George Tomashevich (professor of anthropology, Buffalo State University College)
- Valentin Turchin (Russian dissident; computer scientist, City College, City University of New York)
- Sherwin Wine (rabbi, Birmingham Temple, founder, Society for Humanistic Judaism)
- Marvin Zimmerman (professor of philosophy, State University of New York at Buffalo)

15 NEW RELIGIONS: RASTAFARIANISM AND HARE KRISHNA

Rastafarianism

Origins of Rastafarianism

Rastafarianism, which began in the 1930s in Jamaica, West Indies, is both a religion and a cultural movement.

Rastafarians believe that Haile Selassie (Ras Tafari), Ethiopia's last emperor, is the Messiah. They believe he is the fulfillment of the biblical prophecies of the future Lion of Judah, the Conqueror. As the lion is the king of all beasts, so Haile Selassie is the king of all kings. Rastafarians do not believe that Haile Selassie is dead. They worship him and regard him as their leader.

Rastafarian beliefs

The Bible

"Rastafarian beliefs have their roots in the Bible, but are also influenced by many African traditions and beliefs."
Haile Selassie (1892–1975)

The 12 tribes

Rastafarians think of Ethiopia as the ancient Promised Land spoken of in the Old Testament. They believe that they are one of the original 12 tribes of Israel and look forward to the day when they will return to Ethiopia.

Worship of *Jah*

Rastafarians do not have any churches. When they meet with fellow Rastafarians for prayer, they pray to God who they call *Jah*.

Reggae music

Rastafarianism has greatly influenced Reggae music, so much so that Reggae is now identified with Rastafarian culture and beliefs.

This music developed in the 1960s among the poor people of Kingston, Jamaica. It drew on American soul music developing its own offbeat rhythm. Many of its songs promote the beliefs of the Rastafarianism religious movement. Its most famous performer was Bob Marley (1945–81).

Dreadlocks

Some Rastafarians do not cut their beards. Others leave their hair uncut allowing it to develop into long twists, called dreadlocks, which are meant to inspire "dread" or respect.

These practices fulfil an instruction found in Leviticus 21:5: "Priests must not shave their heads or shave off the edges of their beards or cut their bodies."

F.A.Qs

Q: **How many Rastafarians are there?**
A: There are just under 200,000.

Q: **Where do Rastafarians live?**
A: Mainly in the West Indies, but also in the USA, Canada and the United Kingdom.

Hare Krishna

Origins of ISKCON

The International Society for Krishna Consciousness (ISKCON) is the official name of the Hare Krishna movement founded in 1966 by Bhaktivedante Swami Prabhupada, a Hindu holy man.

Swami

The man who became known as his Divine Grace A. C. Bhaktivedanta Swami Prabhupada, was born in 1896 in Calcutta. He first met his spiritual master, Srila Bhaktisiddhanta Sarasvati Gosvami, in 1922. His master immediately said to Swami, "You are an intelligent young man. Why don't you preach the message of Lord Krishna in English?" This request became the driving force of Swami's life.

In September 1965, Swami traveled to the USA, arriving with no money, but within a year he had managed to establish the International Society for Krishna Consciousness.

During Swami's 12 years of traveling he circled the globe 14 times. As a result of his lecture tours, the Society grew into a worldwide confederation. By the time of his death on November 14, 1977 there were more than one hundred asramas, schools, temples, institutes, and farm communities.

Among famous people influenced by the Hare Krishna movement were the British pop group, the Beatles. It had a particular influence on George Harrison who, on his death in December 2001, requested that his ashes should be interred in India.

Hare Krishna practices

Swami taught his followers to:

- break free from the material world (many male followers therefore shave their heads as a sign of purity and detachment from the cares of the world);
- focus on inner peace through greater self-awareness;
- give up drugs, gambling, drinking alcohol and eating meat;
- chant the names of Hindu gods, Krishna and Rama, in a quest to become united with God.

Chanting

Followers of the movement are transported into "transcendental consciousness" by means of the transcendental vibration established by chanting the holy names of Krishna: *hare krishna, hare krishna, krishna krishna, hare hare rama, hare rama, rama rama, hare hare.* While in this "trascendental consciousness" the struggle against the material is replaced with eternal Krishna consciousness. This is achieved with the assistance of eight transcendental ecstasies:

- being stopped as though dumb
- perspiration
- standing up of hairs on the body
- dislocation of voice
- trembling
- fading of the body
- crying in ecstasy
- trance.